THE
NEW
CELIBACY

Revised and Updated

THE NEW CELIBACY

A JOURNEY TO LOVE, INTIMACY, AND GOOD HEALTH IN A NEW AGE

Gabrielle Brown, Ph.D.

McGRAW-HILL PUBLISHING COMPANY

New York   St. Louis   San Francisco   Auckland   Bogotá
Hamburg   London   Madrid   Mexico   Milan   Montreal
New Delhi   Paris   São Paulo   Singapore
Sydney   Tokyo   Toronto

1 2 3 4 5 6 7 8 9 FGR FGR 8 9 0 9

ISBN 0-07-008439-4

LIBRARY OF CONGRESS CATALOGING-IN-PUBLICATION DATA

Brown, Gabrielle.
  The new celibacy.

  Bibliography: p.
  1. Sexual abstinence.   2. Sexual abstinence—Religious
aspects.   I. Title.
HQ800.15.B76   1988   306.7   88-32581

For you who have opened my heart
and touched me with the grace
of your love

Contents

Preface

In 1978 I began writing a book about celibacy with the hope that it would be of some interest to those individuals pursuing new paths to intimacy in relationships. I didn't have any particular personal flag to wave either for or against celibacy, but I had come to believe that sexual activity ought to be understood for what it really is—a conscious, voluntary behavior which is learned, rather than an instinct over which one has no choice. Understood in this way, celibacy is not the opposite of sexuality, but its "resting state." It is simply the containment of sexual energy, rather than its active expression.

America in the sixties and seventies offered the whole range of perspectives on human sexuality; the subsequent emergence of celibacy within the secular realm was not as surprising as it might at first have seemed. Indeed, it may have been inevitable. There had never been a culture in world history where active sexual behavior for both men and women was so completely unregulated by societal and religious dictates. For better or for worse, there was nowhere else for the pendulum to swing but back.

As I researched celibacy, I spoke with a number of people who were quietly celibate and I began to understand the underlying reasons for their seemingly unusual orientation. During these interviews, some of which eventually appeared in the book, both single and married men and women expressed concern that an overemphasis on sex had begun to harm the development of deeper levels of feeling and relating. As a result, they felt they were missing a reliable foundation for intimacy.

As I was halfway through writing what I thought would be a fairly esoteric manuscript on the history of celibacy and the varieties of celibate love, I started noticing newspaper articles and TV shows which were focusing on, as the *New York Times* put it, "the wave of asexuality" that was beginning to "sweep the nation," initially among the "celebrity chic." In addition, there were a number of reports from therapists and sex educators who were finding that "lack of interest" was the number one sexual concern of their clientele.

I began to realize the truth of the dictum that ideas emerge in the world not due to a single person thinking a single thought, but due to what has been called "group" or "collective" consciousness—what Ralph Waldo Emerson called "the mind of the world." It occurred to me that a growing interest in celibacy must indeed be a collective thought, not just my interest. But then, as the idea took off, my role was apparently to represent it publicly.

By the end of 1982, two years after the publication of *The New Celibacy*, I had appeared as the "celibacy expert" on over 200 TV and radio shows, been interviewed by dozens of newspaper reporters from Chicago to Bangkok, watched the book find its way in translation all over the world (including a Japanese edition with the startling title, *How Not to Sex*), and received hundreds of letters from celibate individuals and couples from everywhere. Here was an idea whose time had indeed come, yet I must admit no one was more surprised than I to find myself its champion.

It has been said that nature always presents a problem and its solution at the same time. I was asked to be on the first national talk show about the new celibacy at the end of June 1980, even prior to the publication of the book. Without overdramatizing this point, I think it is significant that the show coincided with the date of the Gay Freedom Day parade in San Francisco, June 29, 1980, which Randy Shilts, author of *And the Band Played On: Politics, People and the AIDS Epidemic*, identifies as the moment when people began to realize that the disease of acquired immunodeficiency syndrome (AIDS) had arrived in the United States. I recently spoke to him about that odd cultural crossover, and we realized that perhaps some subtle awareness of sexual danger on the part of many participants in the feast of sexual freedom may have sparked interest in a topic which at the time seemed irrelevant. This seems to be at least a partial answer to the question I posed in 1980: "What would anyone be doing as a celibate *now*—at the grand finale of the sexual revolution? That would be like going on a diet just when the banquet was finally served."

It would of course be a mistake to look for a single cause of a growing social trend. In the sixties, the sexual revolution may have been aided by the newly available contraceptive pill, but no one would argue that the Pill was the sole cause of the new sexual abandon. It is clear that long before the fear of AIDS began to deter casual sexual encounters, we were already going in the direction of less sex and more responsible relationships. The era of the one-night stand was already over by the early 1980s. Masters and Johnson's latest research supports this: "The pendulum was already swinging back from extreme indulgence and experimentation."[1]

And, as I discovered, by the late 1970s a significant number of people were already benefiting from both long and short periods of celibacy. So even though today AIDS and other sexually transmitted diseases dramatically emphasize the need for awareness of the possible physical consequences of sex, the fact that secular celibacy was already being practiced a decade ago indicates a different kind of awareness, our becoming conscious of the emotional and spiritual consequences of so-called sexual freedom. I believe this rising consciousness was connected to another, equally important trend occurring at the time—the growing number of Americans seeking paths to self-development via Eastern spiritual practices and through a return to the deeper values of their Western social and spiritual traditions. This trend may well have accounted in part for the concurrent renunciation of superficial, casual sex.

For these individuals, the benefits of celibacy were a positive life choice. They chose it not to avoid the dangers of sex, which were not obvious at the time, but to find a way to further their own inner growth. They seemed to recognize that in order to experience maximum love and intimacy in relationships and even overall good health, a balanced physiology is needed and that overindulgence in anything, including sex, is probably not a good idea. This was, and continues to be, the best basis for understanding and experiencing celibacy. This is all I wanted to convey in the original edition of *The New Celibacy*. But it caused a much bigger stir...

Before I made my first appearance on TV to talk about celibacy—on the now defunct *Tomorrow* show—I was warned that the host, Tom Snyder, might be nasty and sarcastic to me. He wasn't; he was respectful and asked good questions. Far more uncomfortable were his other guests that night, who included the ultraconservative, antifeminist Phyllis Schlafly. She asked me whether I was for celibacy or against it. When I answered that I was "pro-choice," this set off some political, linguistic rockets in her head and she wouldn't speak to me or even look at me after that. There was also "Disco Sally," a seventy-four-year-old "disco swinger" who wore sneakers and was in love with a twenty-four-year-old. They were to be married the next day—celibacy was apparently the last thing on her mind. On a more congruent note, there was the actress Patricia Elliot, who was starring in *The Elephant Man* on Broadway and who had been celibate for five years. She was loving, open, and obviously radiant as she spoke about the benefits of this choice in her life.

A week later, the producers of the *Donahue* show asked me to be a guest with the hope that I could find some celibate individuals to speak out about their experiences. One of the men I had interviewed for the book consented—an extremely

bright, warm, and attractive thirty-four-year-old. By the time
he had finished explaining how he had gone from a divorce
to becoming very actively promiscuous, to recognizing the emptiness of that lifestyle, to becoming celibate for four years, to
meeting his future wife and their decision to save their most
intimate sexual experiences "for our wedding night," nearly
every woman in the audience was breathing sighs of Harle-
quin rapture. Nearly every man, on the other hand, was thoroughly confused, disbelieving, and annoyed. There was also
a young married couple who were being celibate for a time,
in order to keep the more tender and romantic aspects of their
relationship alive. They were obviously in love, clear about
who they were, and articulate. No one was selling celibacy—
it was simply presented as a private matter, a personal consideration. Phil was supportive of all of us and managed to
orchestrate a profound and thoughtful show. It all seemed
very innocent. At one point, however, I found myself counseling a telephone caller on a very sensitive topic in front of
millions of people—what to do when one spouse wants to be
celibate and the other doesn't. At that moment, it dawned on
me that being "an expert" was a real responsibility. From then
on, I knew I had to become more serious regarding the issues
the book was raising.

There were hundreds of other shows, telephone interviews, and interviews with newspapers in the United States
and in Europe, where this new American concept was considered highly fascinating. What *I* found fascinating was that
the questions from the *Louisville Courier* were the same as those
from the *Glasgow Herald*, which were virtually the same as
those from the rest of the media. After a while, I began to
feel as if I were in a long-running play.

Each of these encounters had its own special positive or
negative feeling. Some people were downright furious; others were tremendously relieved. But there were also a lot of
hurting people with real questions. And very touching and
delicate situations continued to arise.

On an L.A. radio talk show hosted by the "other" Michael

Jackson, one caller recounted an experience of sexual abuse he had endured at a Catholic boy's school nearly sixty years ago. When Jackson asked him what the incident had to do with celibacy, there was silence. The caller still wasn't prepared to indict the "celibate" priest who had caused him such anguish. I wanted to suggest that he finally look for professional help, but by then the next caller was on. Here was another moment in which I realized the extent to which one must take responsibility for what one stirs up.

But the opportunities for real, caring, informative discussions were almost nonexistent. It was mostly a ride through Media Land, light-hearted, mostly tongue-in-cheek, a quick dip in the market, but no real exchange. During the *Merv Griffin Show*, I was on the set with two 300-pound sex therapists who unintentionally proved that Freud was quite wrong: Eating is not necessarily sublimated sex or vice versa. There was also a very outspoken older woman sex therapist who had neither Dr. Ruth's sense of humor nor her ability to inform, whose main event seemed to consist of highly titillating remarks which had to be constantly bleeped. And there was *Cosmopolitan* magazine editor Helen Gurley Brown. We two talked for a long while backstage. She seemed overly nervous for someone so often in the public eye. I thought how strange it was that this naturally sweet, shy, and reserved woman, "mouse," as she calls herself, had to represent Big Bold Sex. She commented on how lovely she thought I was, how sad it was for me to have to deal with celibacy, and how she would take it upon herself to help me meet men.

I was the final guest to be introduced, with four minutes of the show remaining. I felt like the Zen punch line to an hour-and-a-half-long off-color joke. The audience had been turned on by the sexual content of the show, and I was offered up as the cold shower. When I arrived on the set, Merv asked me: "So how do you go about becoming celibate? Do you just cut it all off one day?" "You don't have to go that far," I replied. "You just stop having sex." I had learned to be humorous and mild in the face of the odd and sometimes angry reactions I encountered.

This knowledge came in handy when I went on *Late Night with David Letterman*. Neither David nor I understood why we were together alone in front of the cameras. David was ready for Dr. Prim Spinster, and when I wasn't exactly that, nor its opposite, he became confused and uncertain as to whether he could make fun of me or not. He asked how long I'd been celibate; I answered by looking at my watch. It seemed like the only way: Combat the possibility of ridicule with humor. And it worked. David was not pleased, but I made it through without a major loss of dignity.

I was even invited to appear on *To Tell the Truth*, one of my favorite shows from childhood, now off the air. Never in all my life did I think I would do something offbeat enough to warrant being a "contestant" on this show. But writing a book about celibacy was apparently odd enough. While I sat with two "mock" Gabrielle Browns, the announcer read from an "affidavit" which declared that one of us had written a book about men and women who did not have sex all the time. We stumped two of the four panelists. I was sent some contestant prizes, including a selection of French-cut jeans, so fitting for a celibacy maven; actually, too fitting for anything *but* the boudoir.

In 1980, celibacy was considered a "countertrend" but a significant one in that everyone seemed to want to know about it. Today, in an age of concern about the outcomes of sexual activity, along with the continued growth in our understanding that sexual activity is always a conscious choice, celibacy is no longer a countertrend; it has passed into the mainstream and for many of us has become a lifestyle.

Chastity is a wealth that
comes from abundance of love.
Rabindranath Tagore

Celibacy Goes Mainstream

CELIBACY TODAY

What Celibacy Is and What It Is Not

Celibacy originally meant the state of not being married. But those were the days when being single and not having sex were generally synonymous. I use the term the *new celibacy* in a broader sense, to define a psychophysical state, without reference to marital status or any other sociological factors. It can thus be chosen by people who are alone for either social or spiritual reasons or by those who are dating, who are in relationships, or who are married. Although celibacy is most obviously defined as a physical state, the new celibacy is usually accompanied by a certain mental and emotional outlook through which the experience of celibacy can be fully enjoyed. As one man explained it, "There's a real difference to me between celibacy and abstinence. Abstinence is a response on the outside to what's going on, and celibacy is a response from the inside."

So what is this psychophysical state? First of all, it *is* a sexual state. While it's true that it is experienced as not having sex, celibacy is not "asexuality." It does not mean not having sexual feelings, although the patterns of sexual response may change profoundly. In this way, perhaps we can best think about celibacy as *the rest state of sexuality*, where the sexual response becomes more diffuse, expanding in many directions beyond a simple genital response.

To be celibate, one reorients oneself to another way of dealing with sexual feelings; it is an active, not a passive, state. These feelings may shift to any number of physical energy states which can pertain to the mind, to the heart, or to a general state of well-being. And for some people, whether in formal religious life or not, celibacy can serve as part of a path to transform sexual energy into a "higher" form of psychophysical energy leading ultimately to the permanent state of perfect mind-body coordination also known as enlightenment.

On a more mundane level, celibacy has some very practical benefits. We know that although celibacy is not a cure for any sexually transmitted disease (STD), it is certainly a *preventative* measure. But also, interestingly, many individuals feel that celibacy offers a basis for general health that can alleviate some aspects of disease even after infection. And, as we shall see, beginning research suggests that reducing sexual activity and the accompanying stimulation of high hormonal levels within the body may strengthen the immune system.

In addition, from a psychological point of view, celibacy can serve as an *antidote to sexual addiction*, because it can help in dealing directly with the underlying cause of the problem, where the real yearning for intimacy is almost never satisfied through sex. True, under some circumstances, celibacy can be a repression of sexuality, leading to a diminished response to life and personal growth. But generally, if it is chosen for positive reasons, it can have quite the opposite effect, whether such effects are social or spiritual or health-related.

The Changing Sexual Landscape

As discussed, celibacy may have started to emerge as an option at the time it did because there may have been a subtle collective awareness that sex was somehow becoming, if not dangerous, at least in need of more careful consideration. In those days, when sex and love were uniquely perceived as "free," celibacy was both a very radical and a very conservative concept.

"Free" had its own special meaning in the sixties and seventies. It implied no commitments, no responsibilities, as well as freedom from the fears of earlier eras, when single motherhood, abortion, and easily obtained knowledge about birth control and disease control were all generally unsupported by American society.

Today, we are seeing not a complete reversal to the pre-sixties values, but a return of sex to a more social and less individual concern, where physical desire is considered in a context. When you have to take someone's sexual history before making love, the impulse to "do it if it feels good" has nowhere to go. So nowadays, sex is necessarily experienced as a real choice. And, in this sense, AIDS and other STDs are responsible for making *sex today a far more conscious experience for a far greater number of people.*

And so although we are certainly living in a more accepting era than existed thirty years ago, we are simultaneously more aware of both the pleasures *and* the dangers of sexual activity. And obviously, awareness of the dangers has totally restructured our evaluation of promiscuity.

As Randy Shilts, the *San Francisco Chronicle* reporter who has been most closely following the effects of AIDS in the gay community, points out in his book, *And the Band Played On*, the collective concern about AIDS in San Francisco's gay community in 1983 "fueled the most dramatic shift in behavior since the contemporary gay movement was forged in the Stonewall riots of 1969. Nonsexual alternatives thrived.... This new toned-down gay life-style had started as a vogue in early 1983; but by the end of that year it was a trend; in the year that followed, it would turn into a full-scale sociological phenomenon."[1]

It is important to understand that AIDS struck the gay male community not because homosexuality promoted such a thing, but because promiscuity created conditions for the spread of disease. It would just as easily have spread heterosexually had women been as willing as men, wrote Shilts:

> The attraction to promiscuity and depersonalization of sex rested on issues surrounding a fear of intimacy *...These were not gay issues but male issues.* Promiscuity was rampant because in an all-male subculture there was nobody to say "no"—no moderating role like that a woman plays in the heterosexual milieu. Some heterosexual males privately confided that they were enthralled with the idea of the immediate, available, even anonymous sex a bathhouse offered, if they could only find women who would agree. Gay men, of course, agreed, quite frequently....With increases in prevalence outpacing changes in behavior, it appeared that the typical gay man who participated in any risky sexual behavior stood a greater chance of contracting the AIDS virus.[2]

While the advent of widespread, life-threatening disease hastened the dramatic changes in sexual behavior which have been coming up since the seventies, it seems clear that we must also examine this new era and the consequent rearrangement of social interactions it entails apart from the fear-of-illness factors.

Basically, it would be wrong to identify AIDS and other STDs as the sole reason that people are being a great deal more conscious and discriminating about sexual activity. Writes Erica Jong: "The AIDS plague has so fed into America's current need to disown the sexual revolution that it has been hard to determine whether the new disease is just a convenient excuse or truly a new Black Death."[3]

The real topic for discussion might be: When the hoped-for cure for AIDS is found, will we return once again to promiscuous sex? Anecdotal evidence suggests that the answer is no.

Shilts notes that although the whole way of sex as recreation among homosexual men changed dramatically over the decade, it did not happen solely because of AIDS:

> Perhaps the apex of sexuality in the gay community was 1977–1978. At that time no one was saying no to anything. But then a shift occurred, perhaps most clearly around 1984. I think the trend to celibacy started before AIDS. It was a sociological reaction to the excesses of the seventies. It left one empty. People were spent. It was a physically gratifying but not psychically fulfilling way of relating. You can only do that so much until you begin to think there's something wrong here.[4]

In a recent article on the "new sexual realism," one woman remembers the emptiness of sex a decade ago. "What I discovered in the seventies wasn't the wonderful joy of sex but the joylessness of it." She, like many others, gave up casual sex "long before the AIDS and herpes threats were publicized." And New York psychotherapist Nancy Edwards notes, "AIDS has given people the excuse they needed to do what they wanted to do all along—be more sexually discriminating."[5]

Similarly, as Barbara Ehrenreich, coauthor of *Re-Making Love: The Feminization of Sex,* notes: "The backlash against sexual promiscuity was well established before AIDS became a topic of general concern. When it did, it was all too easy to use the tragic new disease to reinforce the developing sexual conservatism."[6] Ehrenreich and others are wary of a conservatism that might employ the tragedy of AIDS to repeal important gains in sexual self-acceptance by women and both self- and social acceptance for homosexuals. The uneasy alliance between right-wing conservatives, the feminist Women Against Pornography groups, and a growing number of fearful individuals concerned not only for themselves but for their children speaks of a nation as confused about issues of sexuality as it has ever been.

While we are not returning to a presixties sexual mentality, it seems that we *are* returning to long-term and committed relationships. Instead of wondering, Who can I sleep with? we now wonder Who can I love?" This is one significant benefit of the new celibacy that we will be exploring throughout this book.

But before we do, let's look at the current signs of the times.

Signs of the Times

In an article in *Ebony* magazine entitled "The New Sexual Morality," the author observed that in this era, when "casual sex can be a death sentence,... anonymous sex with a stranger is almost a thing of the past... and sexual exploits are no longer a glorified topic among men and women."[7]

Here's how the "new sexual realism" is now showing up in our society:

According to a 1988 annual "sex survey," reported in Canada's *Maclean's Magazine*, between 1987 and 1988 there was a 20 percent decrease in the "somewhat active" category, a 50 percent increase in those having less frequent sex, and a 25 percent increase in those giving up sex entirely.

And although fear of AIDS increased behavioral changes in sex for 40 percent of the respondents, it still did not account for all changes in all categories.[8] (Two years earlier, in 1986, there was a 15 percent drop in the sexual activity of those self-described as very active, but there were virtually no dramatic changes in other categories.)

According to a longitudinal study on sexual attitudes conducted by research psychologist Srully Blotnick:[9]

- The number of women opting for celibacy has quadrupled in the past ten years, up from 2 to 3 percent to a current figure of about 10 percent.

- Far fewer women would opt to have casual sex (sex with someone they don't love) in the mid-1980s (28 percent) than would have had casual sex in the 1960s (43 percent) or the 1970s (37 percent).

- In 1980, it was estimated that less than one half of 1 percent of men were celibate. By 1986, that number increased eight-fold to 4 percent. Today it may be as high as 8 percent among heterosexual men and around 10 percent among homosexual men.

- Interest in casual sex among all males similarly decreased by one-third in a decade, from 74 percent in the 1970s to 48 percent in the mid-1980s.

In a recent cover story on AIDS and the single woman, *People* magazine reported the results of its national survey of single women aged 18 to 49: Seventy-five percent were very concerned about AIDS; 40 percent said their sex lives had been directly affected. And even though very few cases of AIDS have occurred beyond the known risk groups (male homosexuals and bisexuals and intravenous (IV) drug users and their sexual partners), the national trend is toward a far more careful sexual lifestyle for all women. They are now choosing partners who are either older, recently divorced, and/or men they have known for a long time.[10]

Beyond the statistical results of attitudinal and behavioral changes, real-life experiences are very different as well. For example, impulsivity is very much on the wane. As one typical result, singles-bar owners who could remember full parking lots "on Sunday mornings from cars left behind the night before" observe that "now there are just a few cars." In fact, most aspects of the Saturday night date are not quite as "cool" as before; dating now requires conversation about condoms, intravenous drug use, homosexuality, bisexuality, or blood transfusions for illnesses such as hemophilia.

One social consequence of this "decasualization of sex" is

that the ritual of courtship is back. It's a time for a "return to romance," an interesting change which implies that romance requires less rather than more sex. Physical intimacy now occurs usually only after a couple has dated for a while, and then it could be a long period of kissing and hand-holding. Said one man, "That first kiss doesn't necessarily come with the first date anymore. And sex on the first date is out of the question for me."[11]

A former "playboy type" has noticed that he angers his dates by openly discussing his sexual history with them and expecting them to do the same: "I finally realized that I was insulting these women by assuming that they had been sexually active, as I had been.... I've discovered that quite a few women have either been abstaining from sex or involved in monogamous relationships."

He's right. "There was a time," recalls one woman, "when I might meet a guy and sleep with him in the same evening, if he was nice and professional and we clicked. But those days are gone forever. It was foolish then, and it's life-threatening now. I'm no closer to marriage than I was 10 years ago, but my attitude toward dating has matured considerably."[12]

Even among monogamous married couples who need not be fearful of disease, there is a significant decrease in sexual activity. According to a recent *Redbook* survey, over 40 percent of married women have sex once a week or less compared with a similar survey taken in 1974 when the figure was 28 percent.[13] Overall, women in the eighties seem less interested in sex even when it's safe. A few years ago, in a well-publicized survey, columnist Ann Landers asked her readers what they wanted most out of a physical relationship with their spouses: The results indicated that the vast majority of women were far more interested in the intimacy of touching and holding than in more specifically sexual activities.

Indeed today, when given a choice, both men and women are opting to use their leisure time for activities other than sex. In a demographically weighted study of 1550 respondents, the D'Arcy, Masius, Benton, and Bowles ad agency found that when the respondents were asked what gives them a "great deal of pleasure and satisfaction," 68 percent choose TV, 61 percent friends, 59 percent helping others, 58 percent vacations, 56 percent hobbies, 55 percent reading. Sex came in at 42 percent, nearly tied with food at 41 percent. The study concluded that today, more people find more pleasure in watching TV, helping others, reading, and in pursuing their various hobbies than in having sex.

The Impact of AIDS and Other STDs

Even as we reflect upon lifestyle changes independent of the fear of AIDS, there is no minimizing the sexual dangers of our time or their impact on our lives.

In 1987, the Centers for Disease Control (CDC) reported that some 12 million people each year are infected with STDs, up 33 percent or four million since 1980. In addition, some 20 million individuals are said to be infected with genital herpes, and an estimated six million with chlamydia, an infectious, debilitating yeast condition. But among the many identifiable sexually transmitted diseases, none is more frightening or more devastating than AIDS.

As of early 1988, according to the CDC, there were over 50,000 adults diagnosed with AIDS in the United States. Another 1.5 million Americans may have the human immuno-deficiency virus (HIV), which could eventually manifest as AIDS. According to Dr. William Haseltine of Harvard Medical School, 270,000 cases of AIDS are predicted in the United States by 1991, with the vast majority of cases to be found among homosexual and bisexual men, hemophiliacs, and IV drug users and their partners.[14]

And even though by now the large homosexual populations in cities such as New York, Los Angeles, and San Francisco have generally been well educated about AIDS and safe sex practices, thereby dramatically curbing the spread of the disease to nearly 0 percent for new cases, the number of incipient AIDS cases will continue to rise for some time. The

National Academy of Sciences has estimated, for example, that half the male homosexual population of San Francisco will become AIDS victims during the next five years as the disease expresses itself over the long term.

At this time, the spread of AIDS in the heterosexual population is occurring primarily among IV drug users and their sexual partners, generally in poor, urban areas and has not reached large numbers among the middle class.[15] But according to Dr. Mathilde Krim and the CDC's Dr. Harold Jaffe, this may be a temporary situation, not a cause for less concern and less vigilance among those not yet infected.[16] We don't know, says Jaffe, what will happen over the next fifteen or twenty years among the general population. At present, it is estimated that globally, as many as five million individuals could contract AIDS.

Simple education pays off greatly. In a 1988 article in the *Journal of the American Medical Association*, Dr. Norman Hearst and Dr. Stephen Hulley of the University of California at San Francisco reported that the chance of heterosexual transmission of AIDS is 1 in 500 for a single act of unprotected intercourse with an infected partner and 1 in 5 billion for a single act where a condom is used and both partners have tested negative for the AIDS virus.

But where AIDS education is far more removed from those who most need to hear the message, i.e., among the IV drug users, it is predicted that AIDS will continue to move through the urban ghettos which breed drug use. In this population, the precondition for the epidemic spread of AIDS is another epidemic disease, the disease of drug addiction. It carries AIDS far afield from sexual activity, to the pediatric hospitals and their infant wards.

In New York City, for example, according to a *New York Times* report in January 1988, one out of sixty-one babies tested positive for AIDS, even though most of their mothers did not know they carried the virus because they were not themselves ill. Thus, not only have AIDS and other STDs surfaced with a vengeance, but the most innocent members of society are being affected. Another population potentially vulnerable to AIDS could be young teens. A recent Planned Parenthood survey found that one out of nine youngsters aged fourteen and under have had sexual intercourse. These youngsters may be the most important target for campaigns to obliterate the spread of AIDS.

Beyond considerations of who is specifically at risk, we all, both as a society and as a world, bear the overwhelming sadness of personal, social, and economic loss. As a result, reported a *Times Mirror* survey conducted by Gallup, between two-thirds and three-quarters of all voters favor increased government spending for AIDS research. And, in a recent poll of 500 college men and women newspaper editors, AIDS was selected as the most pressing issue facing this generation. So no matter who we are or where we live, we are all changing our sexual attitudes and behavior to some degree.

Safer and Monogamous Sex

Even with the lower than predicted incidence of AIDS among heterosexuals and the far lower incidence of new cases in the homosexual communities, the educational campaigns for safe sex are of major importance, although they may well have appeared ten years too late, lagging far behind most of the rest of the world. By early 1987, the only major Western industrialized nation that had not launched a coordinated AIDS education campaign was the United States.[17]

The use of condoms is perhaps the most specific recommendation offered in these campaigns. In this regard, condom machines are now nearly as frequently seen in college dormitories as candy vending machines. In fact, on many campuses such as the University of Kentucky, Boston University, and Dartmouth College, condoms are sold *in* candy machines.

And even though more teenagers are having sex at younger ages and teenage pregnancies have increased, there is apparently more concern among the better-educated younger generation about promiscuity. According to a 1986 survey,[18] 31 percent of today's college students think their parents' generation was too promiscuous. Ten years ago, only 4 percent had thought their parents had been too promiscuous.

Besides safer sex, more of us are returning to monogamy. "I'm not having less sex," reported one twenty-two-year-old woman, "I'm just having it with one person." And a Memphis man acknowledges: "I'm just looking for the woman I can spend the next 40 years with."[19] Similarly, Blotnick's research results indicate that more married couples are staying together: "For the first time since we've been doing our survey, the majority of people we spoke with said they considered their own mate the best candidate with whom to be uninhibited."

And if they don't, they're willing to do something about it. According to Helen Singer Kaplan, M.D., professor of psychiatry and director of the human sexuality clinic at New York Hospital–Cornell Medical Center, there is an increase in the demand for sex therapy for married couples. Couples who would have engaged in adulterous affairs previously are now "afraid to, and they're flocking in for help."[20] Concludes writer Linda Wolfe, it may turn out "to be the best thing to happen to American marriages and relationships in decades....We won't be seeing a return to the days when sexuality was a dark and dirty secret....Rather we'll be seeing more and more instances of people who value their chosen sexual partners highly and are able...to tolerate periods of sexual abstinence."[21]

CHOOSING CELIBACY

Discussions of celibacy are springing up on the news, on talk shows, in print. Many of us can relate to one man's comment: "I've damn near become a monk!" [22] A behavior that seemed so startling in 1980 is now a vital, timely topic. The societal changes in attitudes toward celibacy indicate a meaningful shift from purely sexual expectations to other ways of creating intimacy. And as I noted in an interview with the *Washington Post* several years ago, "Any time a door closes and we think we're going to lose something, another door usually opens and gives us even more freedom."[23]

In an article by Frances FitzGerald on gay life in San Francisco, one man observes:

> It's the "we" generation, not the "me" generation anymore. People look for an inner purpose.... There was a time when we were the cutting edge of commercialism and fashion—that was part of our being—but it's no longer true. Now we're into backpacking and wholesome relationships....
>
> AIDS is a terrible tragedy, yet one that offers real opportunity for personal and collective growth. My friends are taking a new look at their relationships, at the meaning of love and intimacy, and they are making choices.[24]

One choice is of course celibacy, obviously a very viable solution to both the fear of and the reality of contracting AIDS. By now, although safe sex is standard practice in the homosexual communities, which have learned to distinguish between sex and sex that spreads disease, celibacy is a real consideration. With an estimated 10 percent of gay men today practicing celibacy, it is looked upon by Shilts and others "as an option in a spectrum of options, never to be mocked or disparaged, even if it is not for everyone."[25]

For a thirty-two-year-old gay Boston man, it is the only option for now:

> It was very liberating to have the freedom to be sexual as much as you wanted. But now I am not having casual sex at all. I lose interest in spontaneous sex. AIDS is the deterrent for me. Everyone I know is being very careful now. All the couples I know are staying to-

gether. I'm ready for real monogamy and until I meet one man with whom I want to share my life, I prefer to be entirely celibate than to take any risk. I'm testing negative for the AIDS virus and that's a wonderful feeling for me and a great motivation for continuing celibacy.[26]

According to a doctor who works with AIDS patients, "By the time I see them, they have had to decide how to deal with sexual behavior. For some men forced to explore a celibate lifestyle, they begin to appreciate both the intimacy and stability of non-sexual monogamy. To their amazement, they find they can be very intimate with their partners without being sexual."[27]

And even with less reason for concern, many heterosexuals are choosing celibacy. "Let's face it," says one twenty-six-year-old single woman: "Sex just isn't the most important thing in life. I'm certainly not opposed to sex, and I used to enjoy sex, but right now the sanest choice for me is no sex at all. No sex, no worries, no sex, no AIDS. It's really a very simple equation, isn't it?"[28]

Many women feel this way. In 1987, the AIDS hotline in Illinois received 40 percent of their calls from worried women. Director Mary Fleming observed that many of these heterosexual women were "deciding to be celibate." Yet even as we are playing it safe, we'd all like rewards for such good behavior. In *Tales from the Front*, Laura Kavesh and Cheryl Lavin quote one reluctant woman celibate who thinks she might join a convent: "As long as I'm living the lifestyle, I might as well get the credit."[29]

But perhaps most telling is that more of us are choosing celibacy quite apart from the fear of AIDS, for reasons that may prove beneficial in other ways. Some of us are choosing *celibacy as a path to monogamy*. One man in his early forties who was celibate for seventeen months reported that he was "surprised he could live happily without sex." During this period of celibacy, he discovered he had an even more powerful appetite—the desire for a loving, one-woman relationship, which he now enjoys. And even in the context of this relationship, he reports that he is not very sexually active: "I don't need sex—I deny that it is a primary drive. But I do need caring. I can't do without it.... Sex is there but it's not the top of the list." He considers promiscuity dangerous now because of AIDS but also believes that "it was probably almost as dangerous and stupid 20 years ago."[30]

In a "Celibacy Survey" conducted by none other than *Penthouse* magazine, it was concluded that celibacy is "taking on a new respectability":

> Less than half the men and fewer than 40 percent of the women said they were celibate because of fear of disease. And they found benefits in being celibate, particularly emotional and spiritual ones. Seventy-four percent of the women and 68 percent of the men felt that their views of the opposite sex were broadened by the experience. And more than half concluded that being celibate was a healthy thing to do.[31]

(And this from the magazine that the Supreme Court recently ruled had to be taken off the shelves of convenience stores or the stores would be cited for distributing pornography. It is indeed a transitional time!)

Other publications and events support this trend:

- A national magazine, published in Washington, D.C., since 1982, is called *The Celibate Woman*, "a journal for women who are celibate or considering this liberating way of relating to others." It has significantly increased its readership over the last few years.

- A 1988 how-to book on love and marriage includes a chapter on the comeback of celibacy.

- A recent story on National Public Radio described new social clubs springing up on college campuses in California in which the members opt for celibacy as a condition of membership.

- High school classes have begun to discuss celibacy as an alternative to sexual activity: The assumption is that students are already sexually active, but the discussion of celibacy offers a deeper understanding of possibilities than did the repressive denial of the 1950s. For example, a public health class workbook for junior and senior high school students entitled, *Sex Respect: The Option of True Sexual Freedom*, advises students that, even though they may have already been having sex, they can "choose to stop and gain sexual freedom. This choice is called "secondary virginity."[32]

- "When We're Together" and "Detente" ("Wait"), two singles by Tatiana and Johnny, spoke of the virtues of celibacy to teenagers. The records were produced by Johns Hopkins University School of Hygiene and Public Health and funded by The Agency for International Development. They topped the charts in Mexico during the summer of 1986 and sold throughout Latin America.[33]

Moving beyond Psychologized Sex

As celibacy makes inroads into our social lives, it is also becoming part of our psychological makeup. In 1980, we identified a trend toward less sex as "lack of interest." Called "inhibited sexual desire," this was considered the number-one patient complaint in the mental health field. In one study of married couples reported in the *New England Journal of Medicine*, one-third of the couples said they had sex two or three times a month or less; in another study, reported in the *American Journal of Psychiatry*, one-third of the married men and women were sexually abstinent on the average for two months at a time and many for three months and longer.

Noting a growing national trend among both single and married people toward less sex, members of the American Association of Sex Educators, Counselors and Therapists reported that as many as half their patients considered the lack of sexual desire their primary reason for seeking counseling. This was contrasted with previous primary concerns of patients, which had been premature ejaculation, impotence, and inability to have an orgasm—known as "performance criteria." According to these therapists, the *desire* to perform had become problematic, especially among young adults in their twenties and thirties. The patients were said to have good sexual response when they did have sex, but they desired to have it maybe only once every six months. They sought therapy because they felt something was wrong with them and/or that their lack of desire was causing stress in their marriages. Some therapists concluded that there was indeed something to be concerned about. Noted sex researcher Dr. William Masters and Dr. Helen Singer Kaplan, director of the human sexuality program at New York Hospital–Cornell Medical Center, both saw this phenomenon as the result of a generally more open acknowledgment of all sexual concerns. They and some other sex therapists tended to view this reduced sex interest as pathological. They saw it stemming from hostility, depression, anxiety, and other sex-inhibiting neurotic restrictions. Kaplan stated "For some people, sex is fraught with so much anxiety, anger and negative emotion that it may be a better adaptation not to risk it."[34]

But other professionals took a different position. Sex therapist Dr. Shirley Zussman called the new celibacy "a kind of support for saying 'no.'" Researcher-author Shere Hite and psychologist-author Bernard Zilbergeld both noted that neither men nor women either needed or wanted sex all that much. Under the social pressure to be more sexual, many had denied their real desires to move toward less sexual activity, but they regarded their emerging celibate status in a very positive way.

Over the past two decades, from the way we eat to what

we drive, to what we take in from the media, sex has become an inescapable point of reference. Often, though one may not even notice it, there is a tendency to be dominated by sexual thinking to the exclusion of other modes of experiencing. Historians report that this massive sexual liberation is the natural release of a culture which has been horrendously repressed in its sexual life. America has moved from being the most sexually misinformed nation to perhaps the best (technically) informed. Eminently practical, we Americans took to "getting good" at sex with the same intensity with which we once denounced it.

Because sex became *the* methodology for "Total Expression of True Love," love was filtered through a great array of sexual techniques and expectations. Of course, this has been of great benefit to those for whom sexuality was unclear, mysterious, unrewarding, or frightening. In this regard, A. C. Kinsey, William Masters and Virginia Johnson, Shere Hite, and other sex researchers have our gratitude for providing valid, straightforward information regarding sexuality, enabling many people to enjoy sex perhaps for the first time in their lives. This new knowledge provided other ways to think about sexuality. So it was actually less a revolution in sexual activities than one in "thinking about" those activities. Free of guilt, free of embarrassment, why shouldn't we enjoy sex?

Well, we do enjoy sex. But maybe we don't enjoy it as much as we are expected to. The focus on sex means that we are continuously bombarded with all kinds of mirages of fulfillment. This leads to what sex researchers John Gagnon and William Simon call in their book *Sexual Conduct,* "an overenriched conception of sexual behavior." *People end up thinking they are more sexual than they really are.* And they feel they should live up to a false picture of sexuality that has been created as a standard.

The role of sex has also become distorted by its overemphasis in the field of psychotherapy. A large number of therapists tend to encourage patients to dwell on sex at the expense of other, perhaps more pressing, problems. And, in many ways, the psychotherapeutic field has ceased to function as a field but is now a specialization in sexuality. In California, for example, it has recently been ruled illegal for any mental health professional to conduct his or her practice without taking one particular state-sponsored course—a course in sexuality. (No other postcertification course is required).

One result of this narrowing vision is that the majority of people seeking professional help may conclude that their current state of unhappiness is caused by one sexual hangup or another. Since sex is often used to relieve frustration that has occurred in another domain, it is not surprising that many men and women come to view all kinds of frustration as sexual. What may have been a very appropriate area of focus for the patients of Sigmund Freud in the mid-Victorian era has become today an overly significant focus for an already over-sexualized clientele. As a result, there are many people who seek a sexual cause for every personal problem. They conceptualize their unhappiness in sexual terms.

Such people feel that if they could only solve their sexual problems, their lives would become more meaningful and fulfilling. This sexual approach to health and happiness within the therapeutic tradition is very misleading and restricts the potential treatment help. Dr. Harry Stack Sullivan admonished his colleagues, "Let me warn my fellow psychiatrists: If you want to do psychiatry that can well be crowded into a lifetime, see if you can't find something besides the sexual problem in the strangers that come to you for help." And Carl Jung discovered that when patients brought sexual questions to him, they invariably turned out to be spiritual questions.

To combat this overemphasis on sex, philosopher Elisabeth Haich suggests that the study of psychiatry include a personal experience of celibacy. "If a certain period of abstinence was prescribed, purely as an experiment, at universities, Western psychiatry would be plagued by fewer misconceptions!"

Besides its mental health value, we are also led to believe that sex is "good" for us in the same way that healthy foods, exercise, meditation, and other things have been found to raise the quality and longevity of life. But this, too, is misleading. Biologically, we don't lose the ability to be sexual by not being sexual. And unless one is in a very weakened physical condition, one has the potential to be sexual all one's life. Yet the deceptive impression has been created that one must be sexually active to remain healthy. The "use-it-or-lose-it" school of sexologists exploits fears of growing old to the fullest by making it seem as if sexual performance were the true test of youth and aliveness. (Actually, many cultures, particularly Eastern cultures—as will be discussed later—believe that sex can have a *weakening* effect on the physical and mental abilities of people of all ages.)

With this undue emphasis on sex, we may wonder how interested in it we really are.

How Sexual Are We?

It has been found that people don't need or even want sex as much as they think they do. According to the research findings of Gagnon and Simon, "It is demonstrable that sexual activity is in fact not a very powerful drive and the word 'drive' itself may be a misnomer."

Despite the freedom to pursue sexual activity that evolved over the past twenty years, men and women haven't been found by researchers to have become *more* sexual. What has obviously changed are the social/sexual expectations. But, report Gagnon and Simon, the actual intensity of sexual activity has not increased.

In general, sexual response has been understood to be both biologically determined and socially learned. The biological view—best represented in the work of Freud and Kinsey— contrasts with the environmental view. According to sexual-learning exponents Gagnon and Simon, the sociocultural determinants of sexuality replace the biological. They have concluded that it is the nonsexual developments of childhood which lead to sexual development—that sexual activity is not biological or instinctual but socialized. They maintain that sexuality is actually that particular aspect of human development where the triumph of the "sociocultural over the biological level is most complete." And, in fact, there are "numerous social situations in which the reduction and even elimination of sexual activity is managed by greatly disparate populations of biologically normal males and females."

Philosopher Bertrand Russell concurred with this view fifty years earlier when he wrote:

> The word "instinct," in fact, is hardly the proper one to apply to anything so far from rigid as human behavior in sexual matters. The only act in this whole realm which can be called instinctive in the strict psychological sense is the act of sucking in infancy. I do not know how it may be with savages, but civilized people have to learn to perform the sexual act.... What is instinctive... is the impulse to learn it, and often the activity which would give satisfaction is by no means definitely predetermined.[35]

One is ruled neither by the body nor by the mind but by a mutual interaction between the two based on evolutionary processes. It is clear that there is indeed a biological basis for changing sexuality. But although biological considerations are not negated, one could speculate that the biological response of human sexuality is not as fixed or rigid as other biological responses, and in its flexibility, it is more easily influenced by sociological factors. In this regard, as scientist Carl Sagan has noted, the effects of the environment on learning may be extended to affect physiology. As the intellectual experience changes, so does physiology—and vice versa.

So, as our ideas and attitudes toward sex evolve, so do our physiological responses. What one's body desires in the way of a fulfilling experience may become more subtle, more delicate, less specific, less a question of need.

As a possible consequence, sex has been demonstrated to be less interesting to people who are more fully developed in all other areas. In his well-known studies of self-actualized people—people living more of their full potential than the average—Dr. Abraham Maslow found that sex was not a preoccupation within the self-actualized groups:

> Self-actualizing men and women tend on the whole not to seek sex for its own sake....
>
> In self-actualizing people, the orgasm is simultaneously more important and less important than in average people. It is often a profound and mystical experience, and yet the absence of sexuality is more easily tolerated by these people....
>
> Loving at a higher need level makes the lower needs and their frustrations and satisfactions less important, less central, more easily neglected....
>
> These people do not *need* sensuality; they simply enjoy it when it occurs....
>
> Once these lower needs are satisfied, they recede from consciousness, and there is little preoccupation with them.[36]

Dr. Maslow also reported that a self-actualizing person could be sexually abstinent with no harmful effects because he or she would be comfortable with the experience and not feel it as a deprivation.

So if it turns out that most people are not all that interested in sex, especially mature, self-developed individuals, what is the real meaning of sexual freedom? How do we experience deeper growth with regard to our sexuality?

Mental Sex

It is truly mind-boggling to consider what a distance Americans have come sexually from a century ago. What is now

sexually permissible may have been subject to the death pen-
alty back then. Yet the ideal freedom of sexual expression that
has been achieved is still insignificant. This is because sexuality is virtually understood in terms of the physical acts of
sex. "Perversion" in sex is likewise defined by the *behavior* dis-
played by the "pervert." But, in fact, physical sexual activity
is the same everywhere with little real variation. After all, what
can be put where and for how long is pretty much determined
by nature in advance. So in talking about sexual freedom, one
is really talking about mental and social attitudes toward sexuality rather than the physical activities themselves.

There is a very good reason for this. Sex is mostly mental
anyway:

> What really matters are all the ideas and perceptions
> that make sex work effectively for us as individuals.
> ————MASTERS AND JOHNSON

> It is not the body that causes sexual desire...but the
> intellect.
> ————ELISABETH HAICH

> To unveil the flow of thought can...be an even greater
> sexual intimacy than physical nakedness.
> ————ALAN WATTS

A kiss may indeed be still a kiss, but it's usually a promise of
more to come. Without the mental script that accompanies it,
a kiss is not necessarily enjoyable. If you don't agree, try being kissed blindfolded, without knowing who's doing the kissing. The desire to know the giver of the kiss is far more intense
than the experience of the kiss itself.

All sexual activity follows a mental score, a fantasy of
Events to Take Place. And for an event to be sexual, human
beings require far more than the physical acts. (Just ask anyone who has ever been raped.) It is the mental appreciation
and its emotional orchestration that make an event sexual.

Breast and genital examinations and mouth-to-mouth resuscitation generally take place without sexual arousal, but in the right frame of mind, these acts become highly sexual. The mind makes a continuum, a "story," out of a succession of physical moments. So even given a series of potentially sexual physical activities without the necessary mental outlook, "the probability of something sexual happening will remain," note Gagnon and Simon, "exceedingly small."

In fact, sex in some instances is *entirely* mental. Most people have experienced intense sexuality on the level of fantasy without any external stimulation. The body is truly a secondary consideration. A fascinating example was reported by medical researcher Theodore Cole.[37] He found that a number of paraplegic men and women report orgasms reminiscent of those experienced before they became paraplegic—including the entire sexual-response cycle described by Masters and Johnson: excitement, plateau phase, orgasm, and resolution. Dr. Cole goes on to wonder how this occurs if all the afferent impulses to the brain have been interrupted by the spinal-cord injury. He concludes that the orgasm is "psychological" and emphasizes that all "orgasm depends heavily, if not entirely, upon psychological set, whether one is able-bodied or spinal cord-injured."

The fact that sex is predominantly a mental experience through which the body is manipulated means that it is pointless to argue that, as a sexual being, one is at the mercy of one's physiological responses entirely. "The urge to merge" sexually is a thought before it is an action. So in general people decide when it is appropriate to be sexual. In this regard, sex is not only a mental activity, it is also a *voluntary* activity.

As Masters and Johnson have observed, "In one respect sex is like no other physical process. It is the only physical process that can be denied indefinitely, even for a lifetime."

Sometimes we forget that being sexual is a choice. If we are feeling sexy, we may think we have to "do something" about it; otherwise, we'll be repressing an uncontrollable physical urge that will lead to frustration and anxiety. Actually, there is no real need to be sexual so far as human physiology is concerned. If one is, fine; if one is not, fine. The desire will most likely subside. Unlike hunger, thirst, and the craving for intimacy—which are the real needs—physical sexual gratification is far less necessary than imagined.

For an adolescent, especially in our overstimulating society, sex may feel very "involuntary." It is new, it is exciting, it is completely overshadowing. Only gradually does one learn that one has mastery over sexuality just as one learns mastery over many experiences in life. We learn to control sexual behavior and not to be controlled by sexual feelings. We learn that we can choose to be sexual or choose not to be. In *Existential Sexuality: Choosing to Love* Dr. Peter Koestenbaum goes so far as to say: "Human beings are not by nature sexual... but choose to be so. Sex is a natural urge, but the role it plays in your life and the importance you attribute to it...is a matter of free choice."

Yet we are all heavily influenced in this choice. And the reason most of us decide in favor of being sexual as much as possible is because we've been taught that sex is the road to personal fulfillment. This is one of the most destructive myths about sex—that there is such a thing as permanent fulfillment on the sexual level.

No matter how great an orgasm one has or how great an orgasm one's partner has, sex does not bring fulfillment. And if something more deep and permanent is desired in the expression of love and one does not even experience it, one may feel unfulfilled, even saddened by the sexual act. There is a clear psychological description of this feeling called "postcoital tristesse" or "sadness after sex." This may happen because, as Elisabeth Haich observed:

> Sexuality mimics love. It compels tenderness and embraces, it forces the lovers to hug one another, to allay one another's pain through the revelations of sexuality, as when true love is exchanged. What follows such experiences? Disappointments, a bitter after-taste, mu-

tual accusations or bleak loneliness, feelings of exploi-
tation and defilement. *Neither of the two gave true love
but only expected to receive it, therefore, neither received it!*[38]

Many people, believing that sex is the only way to become
fulfilled, spend years searching for lasting happiness in sexual encounters. Such is the loneliness of the sexual seeker who
continues to search for personal liberation in a series of static
encounters. In this fixed pattern of behavior, there is always
a feeling of futility, of going nowhere.

But the positive side of the seeking is the recognition that
one is looking for something more. Obviously, the more you
expect out of sex, the more you expect out of life. In the search
for fulfillment, for a permanent state of happiness and joy,
you may try everything. With each experience, you may be
able to see some progress, at least on the level of understanding. It is this understanding that gives the feeling of growth
and progress.

The Need for More

The desire for growth and progress is really a basic part of
living—no matter what you enjoy, you inevitably want more.
You either have to get better at it, grow in it, or get more of
it. A new dress or sport coat only satisfies for a short time
until something newer to wear is desired. Even fame and success have to be continually renewed to maintain happiness.
In the glory of tomorrow's dinner, tonight's meal is forgot-
ten. The satisfaction of mastering a Beethoven sonata may
evaporate with the upcoming desire to learn a new one.

Similarly, the feeling of progress is necessary in physical
activity. Mastery of the body is an essential part of human
achievement. Just look at how the records set during the
Olympic Games continue to be broken every four years. No
doubt psychological training and mental attitude programs ad-

vance as well, breaking mental boundaries prior to the breaking of physical boundaries. But the body has its limits, and goals are always established within those limits. So physical progress, although necessary and enjoyable, is finite. In fact, many human endeavors are finite. And it is important to evaluate our desire to progress in light of what is possible.

With some things—the ineffables, the open-ended infinites such as love, knowledge, creativity—there's no need to worry. There's plenty of room to grow and expand. But with some things that may seem unlimited but really aren't, one could get stuck trying to break limits in a world of limits until all that is left are pieces of experiences—incomplete and less and less satisfying.

The acts of sex are some of those things. You can only get so good at each act—there are only so many good positions; orgasms can only be multiplied to a certain limit. If we think of sex as a progressive physical activity, as a kind of Olympics in the bedroom where records must be broken and performances judged, sex is really limited to physical performance criteria. Yet even if we don't just limit sex in this way, like other finite experiences, sex requires progressive achievement to continue to be enjoyable. We have to feel we are having better and better sexual experiences, whether with one person or with a series of people. Without this progress, sex seems to lose its value.

Sexually, one can "progress" either with a particular partner toward richer and fuller sexual experiences or with a series of partners toward an increasingly more complex set of sexual experiences heightened by the variety itself.

If one's sexual attention is exclusively on one partner, there may be a kind of subtle progression through a series of detailed learning experiences until one "gets good at" every interesting sexual activity. As one becomes more and more knowledgeable, new experiences are called for—not only to satisfy recurring sexual desires but also to keep progressing in the creation of the sexual relationship.

A person may read all the books on sexuality to learn new

positions and techniques of lovemaking; he or she may travel to exotic places to create new environments for the activities. One may create an environment of exotic erotica right in one's own bedroom with myriad design features installed to reveal new angles of sexual interest. Or one may venture into the College of Multiple Orgasm and achieve numerical Advances in Contraction, and Degrees in Intensity. But sooner or later, no matter how much you love your partner, you are going to get bored once you run out of ways to progress in sexual expression. This may not happen in a week of lovemaking, but it can easily occur after five or ten years of marriage. At that point, a couple may start to question the validity of their relationship—and whether they are really in love.

This is an all-too-common occurrence in marriage. And of course a great and tragic misunderstanding. For if the partners see sexual activity as the key to the entire relationship or even as a reflection of the quality of the relationship, they may convince themselves that the relationship is over, done for. In fact, they may have grown *beyond* the need for sex and the sexual level of relating for a time and it may indicate, as we shall see later, the right moment to start to experience each other on an entirely new plane of union in relationship.

But because of the pressure on a couple to be sexual, they may feel compelled to "open" their marriage to others and look for sexual fulfillment with different partners in order to save the marriage.

Couples seeking further sexual progress as described above or single people looking for the "right one" or individuals seeking fulfillment through constant variety may choose to have sexual experiences with a number of different people. But here, too, progress and learning seem to continue only just so far. Then a person may well become bored with, say, one partner at a time or one partner for more than one night. He or she may branch out to groups of people, new combinations of positions, and so on. The desire to keep having newer and newer experiences may start to replace the quality of each event as the determinant of progress.

Another way to look at this pursuit of fulfillment through sex is to examine what can be called the Thrill Effect—a search for overwhelming excitement in sexual encounters.

Seeking the "Thrill"

"Uninhibited civilized people...may fall deeply in love and be for some years entirely absorbed in one person, but sooner or later sexual familiarity dulls the edge of passion, and then they begin to look elsewhere for a revival of the old thrill." Bertrand Russell's observation is corroborated by modern research. In her studies on romantic love, Dr. Elaine Walster found that "six to thirty months is the average duration of the kind of heart-stopping, I'm-about-to-faint romantic frenzy we all think of as being 'in love.'" Of the ten thousand people Walster questioned, most reported that the intensity of passion starts to diminish after a couple of years at most.[39]

According to several authorities, what many of us yearn for sexually is to re-create or at least reexperience the thrill and ardor of adolescent sexual love. With hearts pounding and pulses racing, adolescents approach sexuality as if approaching a mysterious deity. But, as psychologist Hugo Beigel points out, these "adolescent feelings...though recognized as precious, are rarely experienced in adulthood with the same ardor."

Another interpretation of this search for the thrill is that one mistakes the thrill of fear and anxiety that may have accompanied sex during adolescence for the Thrill itself. According to H.J. Campbell in *The Pleasure Areas: A New Theory of Behavior*, "the initial exquisite pleasure is predominantly autonomic rather than sexual." Thus, when people seek to recapture the excitement of adolescent sex in adulthood, it is not surprising that they fail, particularly if they are halfway over the fear of sex. If one is still fearful, interestingly enough, sex is still thrilling. This may account for the pursuit of new and unusual sexual activities replacing more ordinary pursuits as one grows more complacent about sex.

Some homosexuals have recognized that the more dangerous and sometimes hidden nature of homosexuality adds a dimension of thrill not found in most heterosexual encounters. And danger apparently helps heterosexual romance as well. Walster's study revealed that obstacles to love provide an important spur to passion and romance. The extramarital affair, parental disapproval, and other difficult situations were cited as aspects of love relations structured within external limits that excite longer-term romance. When it is forbidden, it's still thrilling. But as fewer and fewer acts are socially forbidden, eventually the "thrill" is gone.

"Transcendent" Sex

Substituting the sexual for the spiritual or vice versa in the attempt to become fulfilled is another common mistake. Much of Jung's psychoanalytic work explored the deep interconnectedness often experienced between sexuality and spirituality. If one happens to have a spiritual experience during sex, it is easy to confuse the two and conclude that the spiritual can only be recaptured through the sexual. In *Free and Female*, Barbara Seaman describes "transcendent" sex:

> Once an individual has experienced transcendent sex even once, it seems to change her (or him) for a lifetime, making her (or him) more spontaneous, more open, more confident, more loving, more purposeful, more peaceful. Naturally enough, the desire to repeat such an experience becomes very strong. Many "promiscuous" persons are idealists in drag...who are searching—futilely, as a rule—for a replay of some transcendent sexual experience they once enjoyed.[40]

Let's say you have an experience of a transcendental nature that opens you fully and you feel as if you are taken to the far reaches of the universe or you have a strong feeling of timelessness and unboundedness. And let's say that you have this experience during a sexual encounter. Then you may conclude that sex is the sole avenue to the experience of going beyond your everyday boundaries.

In fact, this experience can occur and does occur in many life situations. Artists, business people, scientists, writers—anybody who creates, people who meditate, religious people, young children, and many others have all reported experiences of transcending that often take place in very ordinary circumstances. In her book *Ecstasy*, Marghanita Laski documents a variety of such experiences, as does Maslow in his work on "peak experiences."

These moments of transcendence may indeed occur during sex or they may not. But we do ourselves and our lovers a great disservice if we continue to seek the spiritual experience of unboundedness only in the sexual realm. Because we've been taught to look for the earth to move during sex, we might blindly focus all our spiritual hopes on this one limited channel of experience. And in so doing we eliminate more fruitful paths to obtaining the fulfillment we desire.

But once we become aware that what we are seeking *through* sex is something *other* than sex, we may decide to take attention off sex entirely, in order to explore whatever else is available. This shift in attention occurs naturally as one gains increased satisfaction in other experiences—in the ability to love, in the development of creative expression, in the achievement of success in any activity. As one grows, one inevitably wants to experience the kind of profundity of expression enjoyed in all other parts of life. If the quality of sex doesn't measure up, sex begins to move out of the limelight.

This is a primary reason why people entertain celibacy as a possibility at some time in their lives—because they want to experience and express something closer and more representative of their own nature than even sex. It can be thought of as the desire for something more eternal, more permanent. And when individuals start to desire this fuller kind of self-expression, everything they do has to be reevaluated in light of these new desires.

FROM SEX TO CELIBACY

Celibacy is a state of life known only to humans. The fact that one *can* be celibate if one so chooses is an indication of the growth of freedom. Natural life has evolved from the state of determined sexuality experienced by the lower animals to a state of potential sexuality wherein human beings are free to choose to be sexual or not.

This book is principally addressed to those for whom celibacy may be chosen as a positive life experience, although not necessarily for a lifetime. But it is useful to distinguish among the various reasons for celibate living by describing each briefly.

There are really several kinds of celibacy, each of which has certain physical, mental, and social characteristics. The experience of celibacy is determined by why one has become celibate. In addition, two main categories of celibacy can and ought to be distinguished. One is celibacy freely chosen and the other is celibacy based on repression or fear of sex, what can be called "celibacy by default."

Life Celibates

Generally, when thinking about celibacy, we may think of the life celibate. Such individuals often seem very far removed from ordinary life. As such, "the figure of the celibate monk, the wandering ascetic, the hermit who has renounced the flesh has always impressed, astonished, fascinated, shocked, even outraged the worldly man."[41]

Yet most of our traditional knowledge about celibacy comes from that group of spiritual men and women who have made a total commitment to a celibate life for the sake of a higher goal, often religious in nature.

In certain religions and on some spiritual paths, a person may choose to be celibate for life in order to keep his or her attention on the most elevated levels of knowledge and experience in devotion to God. The purity and dignity of such a deep personal commitment to God found in the various traditions of religious celibacy often serve to inspire the society. In defining celibacy, the *Encyclopaedia Britannica* describes how the uplift of the society is brought about through the example of a spiritual life advanced by the function of celibacy: "The celibate is seen by the community as it would like to be seen by the gods."

The mystique of the life celibates is no doubt enhanced by their seeming indifference to sex in light of what they must be experiencing without sex. Often they appear to have transcended sex entirely. Even Freud, who could never seem to leave a sexually repressed rock unturned, admitted that many life celibates may have grown beyond ordinary sexual needs and desires. He wrote: "What they bring about in themselves in this way is a state of evenly suspended, steadfast, affectionate feeling, which has little external resemblance any more to the stormy agitations of genital love." However, as will be discussed later, not all celibacy in the name of religion produces such spiritually beneficial results.

Other than the religious life celibate, there are also life celibates who have found the rewards of their celibacy applicable to other higher life goals. The naturalist Jonathan Chapman, better known as Johnny Appleseed, is one famous example of a spontaneous life celibate whose life activity was inspired in its dedication to bettering humanity and the environment and, thus, he "sowed his seed" in a more universal way.

Life celibates are usually individuals who are physically, mentally, and socially self-sufficient and who have no real need of other people in order to be happy, even though they may be devoted to helping others. But there is another dimension of celibate living—what could be called perhaps "secular celibacy"—that includes some aspects of religious celibate life and some aspects of everyday social life.

Secular Celibates

Why do certain types of sexual behavior—particularly celibacy and virginity—seem to recur again and again

at "higher" stages immediately after a generation of
supposedly liberated men have come to renounce them?
——HERBERT RICHARDSON

Apart from the solitary life commitment of certain religious
and/or spiritually inclined individuals, celibacy has also been
the basis for a number of "ideal" societies throughout history,
including much of Eastern culture and certain key societies in
Western culture—from Platonic idealism through the courtly
or romantic love tradition of the Middle Ages through some
nineteenth-century American utopian communities to modern times. This history will be explored in the next chapter.
Yet even at present our own society is looking once again toward celibacy—at least on a temporary basis.

It is important to understand that times of celibacy can be
beneficial to most people—even married couples—but that the
benefits are most fully experienced when one has become celibate by free choice. By contrast, there are many of us who are
physically celibate but not necessarily because we want to be.

Celibacy by Default (Or Why the Earth Isn't Moving for Me in San Andreas)

One obvious reason for involuntary celibacy is a lack of suit-
able partners. There are times in everyone's life when there
is simply no attractive potential mate around. A widow, a wid-
ower, or divorcee may go for long periods adjusting to celibacy
before finding another partner. Sometimes celibacy occurs
even though sexual experience is intensely longed for, as in
the case of a young student looking for a first partner or a
"war widow" awaiting the return of her spouse. This can be
called "celibacy by default"—one is celibate, but not by choice.

Another experience of physical celibacy is also by default—
the result of neurotic personality patterns that forbid an individual comfortable participation in any sexual experience.
For such people, the fear of failure, rejection, "sinning,"

"getting dirty," whatever—is too great to allow sexual feelings to be expressed physically. Usually these individuals are immersed in a consuming mental sexual life, and even though they are physically celibate it is certainly not a healthy celibacy.

A third and perhaps most significant reason for involuntary celibacy these days is the fear of the consequences of sexual activity. This is what can be called "fear-based" celibacy by default. If you're celibate because you are afraid of getting ill or of spreading illness to others, it may not feel expansive. It may feel scary and lonely. Perhaps we begin to appreciate the value of celibacy in a fuller and more uplifting context once we realize that celibacy can also be chosen and experienced in a very positive way.

Celibacy by Choice

If one is not free to choose to be sexual, neither is one free to choose to be celibate. Like sex, celibacy is most valuable when freely chosen.

Celibacy and sex are interdependent. To be totally celibate is to be totally sexual, even if unexpressed. One is at home with both experiences but not overshadowed by either. If two people cannot choose freely to be celibate because sex dominates their lives so entirely, then they are not really choosing sexuality freely either. Each act of sex must be a real choice from the status of the fullness of celibacy. If one chooses to express this fullness in sexual activity, fine—but the choice is one's own. If one chooses not to express it in favor of maintaining celibacy, this too is a free choice.

The most important reason for becoming celibate by choice is that we recognize that we want to be. Just as one can decide to be sexual, one can decide to be celibate—for a week or two, for a month, for a year, even for many years.

And how do you know if it might be a good time for you to try a little celibacy? Well, one way to know is when the desire for sex diminishes. If your attention is not on sex, it's easy to be celibate. If, on the other hand, you are always think-ing about sex and full of sexual fantasies, it might not be the right time to be celibate. If you are not ready to be celibate, you could get hung up *trying* to be comfortable in that state and more and more sexual fantasies would be the result.

The best way to tell if you might be ready to be celibate for some time is if it feels natural.

Celibacy When the Time Is Right

Celibacy is not an intellectual idea. It is not an ideal. It is a state of life that may occur in some people in a natural way. If it is more comfortable not to be sexual than to be sexual, then it is a natural kind of celibacy. On the mental level, if one's attention is not on sex, that too is indicative of a natural time of celibacy. Sexual fantasies tend to drop off as one be-comes more celibate, as one's attention moves to other sources of enjoyment in life. If, however, one is physically celibate yet always thinking about sex and full of sexual fantasies, cel-ibacy may not feel natural.

A precondition for being celibate is probably a certain de-velopment in the physiology of the individual. As will be dis-cussed later, research on the effects of celibacy on the immune system is just beginning. But there have been no studies as yet on the physiological changes that occur as one moves from sexual activity to celibacy, although celibate people do report that it becomes increasingly easier to be celibate the longer one remains celibate. On the other hand, there is no evidence to suggest that the *ability* to have sex is ever lost through cel-ibacy. (In fact, short periods of celibacy may be the best cure for sexual problems such as impotence.) What may be lost is the *desire* for sex. As one becomes celibate, one may first lose not one's sexual desires but the *desire for* sexual desire. In this culture, the possibility of losing the desire to have sex may be thought of as akin to quiet death. But nature is much better-natured than that; if the desire to have sex goes, celibate people say, it is because the desire for other important experiences has replaced it.

For some people, becoming celibate means being in control of their lives. A realization may have come that sex is not as enjoyable as they would like, yet they drifted along in sexual activity anyway. But a time may come when the feeling to be true to their own desires enables them to take hold of their own lives and decide to say no to sex for a while. Some of us arrive at islands of sexual activity on a lake of celibacy and then must decide whether to land or not. Others may arrive at islands of celibacy on a lake of sexual activity and must decide to disembark or not and for how long.

Just as people differ in their needs for closeness and distance emotionally, they differ in their needs for sexual closeness or distance at any given time. If one is comfortable with one's sexuality but feels a declining interest in pursuing sexual activity, one must feel free to be celibate. It would not always be good to continue having sex when one doesn't feel like having sex, no matter what social obligations may prevail. If sex has become unfulfilling but one continues to participate, it takes on a character of *unnaturalness*. That means that sex has become an inappropriate means of expression of the personality at that time. If people are expressing something other than what they are or less than what they are at any given moment, they will feel frustrated, less open, less full, diminished, cut off from their feelings.

The fuller levels of feeling, the deep levels of tenderness and intimacy, can easily be lost in sex because sexual activity is so dominating and tends to hold the focus of attention when people are making love. You may yearn to express these deeper parts to your lover but may end up expressing only the sexual. It is then that an individual or a couple may decide in favor of celibacy. It may not be a long period of celibacy—perhaps only a week or two—but it can be just what is needed at the time.

At the very least, celibacy can offer the opportunity for "refueling" sexuality. As pure unexpressed sexuality, the celibate state is the "rest state" of sexuality and, as such, contains the full potential of one's sexuality. But it also contains the full potential of all love experiences as well as other spiritual possibilities. It is in no way meant to deny love; on the contrary, it is meant to revitalize it and rediscover it. As Richardson notes, "The renunciation of sexual activity is not a renunciation of love...rather of that kind of love that has sexual orgasm and procreation as its purpose."

Celibacy can offer an *alternative* approach to love and loving by allowing sexuality to remain at rest in its most delicate and unbounded state. By choosing to be celibate, we actually reestablish the boundaries of our sexuality while, at the same time, we find new and perhaps more subtle ways of expressing and feeling love.

To have new experiences in life, often we have to break certain rigid patterns of behavior in order to free ourselves to enjoy other possibilities that might be lying dormant. In *The Pleasure Areas*, H. J. Campbell points out that for our lives to grow freely, the pathways in the brain have to be continually rechanneled:

> When information is processed by the brain, preferred pathways are established....Only brains that contain preferred pathways can exhibit the characteristics of a mind....If the conditions are right, the same such pathways can be obliterated in favor of new ones....
>
> A person whose behavior is based upon indoctrinated preferred pathways is no less a machine than the computer that behaves according to a preset program....We can only attain individuality, personal freedom and nonmechanical life if we determine our own preferred pathways.[42]

New neural response patterns are easy for us to establish. And we can establish new kinds of response in love, in creating, in perceiving, simply by being celibate.

If something is imposed from the outside, it can become a barrier. But if it is self-imposed—from inside—it can be a means to achievement. In a closed system of behavior, where patterning is fixed and rigid due to fear, anxiety, and psycho-physical blocking, celibacy may appear pathological. In an open system of behavior, where the person has grown beyond the regular needs pattern of a sexual commitment, celibacy may be evolutionary.

Tuning In to Nonsexual Responses

Just as silence is the basis for sound, for speech, for music, celibacy is the basis for sex. The settledness of the celibate state has the potential to give rise to active sexual functioning. Sexual expression can be very gross or very subtle, depending on the feelings and awareness of the individuals involved in the expression; celibacy can be understood in the context of sexuality as the subtlest form of sexuality—potential but unexpressed.

If a person has been playing the stereo constantly for weeks and then turns it off one day, she immediately "hears" the silence, and that silence seems full. Listening more closely, she may even hear in her own head some subtle music that is more charming than what she was listening to on the stereo all that time.

By being celibate, by turning off the "sexual stereo," one may discover a new dimension of response in love, in creation, in perception underneath the sexual program. People may then find that they are able to begin to experience a quality of attention that makes them more tuned in to feelings of intimacy, tenderness, and fullness of love in relationships, as well as in other parts of their lives. Instead of being dominated by just one kind of human love response—the sexual—they are free to experience other responses.

Celibacy is a way of breaking boundaries, old patterns of behavior that exist between the mind and body, between the self and others. It enables one to be free of sexuality in order to evaluate and experience the joys of life without sex. If the results of being celibate for some time lead to becoming sexual once again, fine; it will be bringing about an even more sexually alive state than before. If one chooses to remain celibate because other nonsexual experiences turn out to be very fascinating, then too there will be clear benefits resulting from the celibate exploration.

The Old Celibacy

CELIBACY IN RELIGION

2 The gift of celibacy is, in reality, the call to be a "seer,"...a dedication to others...loving inside a vast reality. This vision is necessary for a celibate to be a well-adjusted and happy person.
——JOSEPH WADE

In the life of the religious, celibacy has long been a spiritual discipline, an exercise for the devotee to advance in spiritual growth. It has been suggested that celibacy offers a way for the religious individual to have his or her attention most purely absorbed in the commitment to seek and experience God.

In the practices of various ancient religions, celibacy was sacerdotal—represented in the power of the shaman, the priests, and the priestesses—wherein sexual power was ritually transformed into religious power. More generally, throughout history, those religious individuals dedicated to spiritual life set themselves apart from the larger society and male and female monasticism was established as a religious lifestyle. Celibacy was practiced to further spiritual goals and perform ser-

41

vice to God in one-pointed, pure devotion. Typically, these individuals have lived both cloistered in groups or solitary— like the hermit, the wandering ascetic, or the priest living a monastic life within the secular community.

The tradition of celibacy is established in about half the major world religions. Interestingly, the tradition breaks the usual division between Eastern and Western cultures. For example, celibacy is traditional in the Eastern religions of Hinduism, Buddhism, Taoism, and Jainism but not in Islam or Confucianism. Likewise, in the West, celibacy is traditional in Roman Catholicism and the Eastern Orthodox Church but not in Judaism or Protestantism.

Hinduism

Of all the world religions past and present, celibacy is most widely practiced in the Eastern religions, particularly in Hinduism. Just as one does not have to be a priest to lead a religious life within Hinduism, one does not have to be a priest to be celibate. The male and female celibate devotees, whether priests or not, are the *sadhus*—the "holy ones."

In the 5000-year-old Hindu tradition, the ideal spiritual life consists of four stages, representing four developmental behavioral stages of ideal human growth. One begins with the *bramacharya* (celibate) life of the young student. Around age ten, the *bramacharin* embarks upon a rigorous training in knowledge in which his celibate status serves as the basis for growing consciousness. He studies, usually with a master, while maintaining celibacy for the next twelve years. This training is followed by a second stage, *garhasthya*—the active daily life of marriage and family. Not all marry at this time; some continue as monks and remain celibate for their entire lives, but most marry and raise families. Both paths—that of the celibate and of the householder—are equally respected in Hinduism.

Of those who have married, some will continue to uphold the spiritual commitment to ideal life and choose to leave active life to become religious recluses during the third stage, *vanaprastha*. Some married couples go together to the forest or mountains, but as celibates, for this third stage is a return to celibate life. It is a time to be free of worldly possessions and family duties and continues into the last stage, *sanyasa*, which requires a life completely alone, the renunciation of all family and friends as well as all material things. The *sanyasin* enjoys silence through meditation and is committed to radiating the purity of his or her highly developed consciousness throughout the universe.

Buddhism

Out of the Hindu tradition of ideal spiritual life came the Buddha—Gautama Siddartha—who 2500 years ago founded the monastic order of Buddhism, which has since come to include both monks and married people. In modern Buddhism in Tibet, Japan, and Thailand, monks are permitted to marry. And married men may spend time as monks prior to and during the course of married life, alternating celibate life with marriage. But the most devout aspirants in the Buddhist tradition emphasize monasticism and long-term celibacy as a foundation of the contemplative life in order to achieve the state known as *arhat*—the state of enlightenment—through the establishment of complete freedom and detachment from material life, including the bonds of sexuality.

The Tantric Tradition

A later Indian tradition, Tantra, came to hold that celibacy was not necessary for the growth of spiritual life. The basic teaching of Tantra is the unity of *nirvana* and *samsara*, the integration of mystical and sensual experience. And, in fact, no real difference is seen between the two. A two-in-one correlation creates the unity of two polar entities into one encompassing whole. These polar energies are most often symbolized in sexual terms. All spirituality in the Tantric tradition is considered based in sexuality: male and female are juxtaposed to create new unity with regard to knowledge, God, and enlightenment.

The Eastern traditions, particularly the Tantric, use the power of sexuality to express spirituality symbolically. In all the so-called erotic literature of the East, one misses the great meaning of the works if the ritual and symbolic content is ignored. By the same token, Eastern celibacy is not merely nonsexuality—nor is it associated with "nonsinfulness" for the sake of being "good" for God.

In the Eastern traditions, celibacy represents a discipline to gain enlightenment, whereby all the physical, mental, and emotional energy of the body, mind, and senses is directed toward progressively higher levels of evolution. The understanding is that to find God, one has to transcend the thought of God; to let the heart be fully opened to God, one has to transcend emotion. In the same way, to be fully spiritual, one becomes celibate—in order to transcend the boundaries of sex.

Western celibacy does not have a tradition of physical and spiritual growth associated with it the way the Eastern traditions do. And the Western outlook on celibacy varies considerably from religion to religion and also within each particular religion. Overall, within the Judeo-Christian tradition, there is a message of procreation that underlies the sexual relationship. "Be fruitful and multiply," was God's dictum. Anything that defies that consideration is thus looked upon with less compassion. This includes men "wasting seed," "barren" women, and sex for pleasure.

Judaism

The ancient tenets of Judaism embraced marriage for all, including the rabbis, who had to be married in order to pursue higher study. (One exception was the unmarried prophet Jeremiah.)

However, the rituals of Jewish marriage were such that

sex was not in the least indiscriminate but very strictly disciplined, permissible only at times when procreation was likely. And, in some cases, in order to study the Torah and other Jewish scriptures, rabbis would ask permission from their wives to be celibate and free of familial concerns in order to devote themselves exclusively to knowledge. But, among the Jewish sects, there was one notable group, the Essenes—who appeared two centuries before Christ—who were known for being celibate.

The Essenes were an ascetic sect associated with the Qumran community from the region around the Dead Sea where the Qumran documents—the Dead Sea Scrolls—were written.

Like the Shakers centuries later, the Essenes were a community of celibates who believed in "control of the bodily passions" for the purpose of cultivating a pure and holy nature. They lived simply, with emphasis on humility, obedience, and purity. They participated in none of the animal sacrifices common to the times. Unlike the Shakers, however, almost all were men. Apparently, although some were married and some celibate only temporarily, most were committed life celibates. They lived in a community of equal fellowship and were said to be intolerant of outsiders and not particularly friendly to women. According to the historian Pliny, the Essenes often participated in family life by adopting young children to raise.

Christianity

Celibacy in the Christian religion has been generally regarded not as a physical discipline to purify the body and enliven consciousness but as an exemplary virtue of devotion to God. Unfortunately, the tradition of celibacy in Christianity has suffered through a history of sexual misunderstanding without much benefit of the knowledge and experience of the value of celibacy to unfold the higher states of experience of God found in the Eastern religions.

For the most part, Christian celibacy has been utilized as

an uneasy refuge for warding off the evils of sexuality, based on the belief in original sin. The Christian concept of original sin (traced to the female, notes historian Barbara Tuchman, "Theology being the work of males") holds that sexual knowledge and experience may prevent one from entering the Kingdom of Heaven after death. So, in order for the individual to be accepted, sexuality must be rooted out—and that is most simply accomplished through abstaining from sexual activity.

But abstinence as a standard of religious devotion hasn't had much success in the 2000 years it has been upheld as an ideal in Christianity.

The issues of celibacy and sex were initially separate from the Christian religion. They were introduced in the belief that with the advent of the New Age heralded by the coming of Christ, the Kingdom of God was at hand and there would be no need for marriage since, in St. Paul's view, "all would be like angels." Jesus was said to have encouraged the single celibate life for his disciples: "Let those accept it who can." Some apostles, like Peter, married but others gave up married life and family responsibilities to devote themselves to the "New Age." A favoring of the single life over married life for the religious came to predominate and eventually marriage, in its association with sex, became something less than fully spiritual in Christianity. As St. Paul wrote in the First Epistle to the Corinthians:

> I would that all men were even as I myself [i.e., celibate]....I say, therefore, to the unmarried and widows, it is good for them if they thus abide even as I. But if they cannot contain, let them marry: for it is better to marry than to burn.

St. Paul, according to Bertrand Russell, saw marriage as the lesser evil when compared with indiscriminate sex. "The Christian view that all intercourse outside marriage is immoral was...based upon the view that all sexual intercourse, even within marriage, is regrettable...and something of a handicap in the attempt to win salvation."

Priest Donald Goergen maintains that the "sin" of sexuality as the enemy of spirituality began with Paul and was magnified by Augustine. Augustine encouraged celibacy in marriage. For him "chastity can be celibate or conjugal, and conjugal chastity is still true chastity. Conjugal chastity limits sexual intercourse quite explicitly to procreation." Tuchman also emphasizes Augustine's abhorrence of sexuality for its own sake. "Using copulation for the delight that is in it and not for the end intended was, Augustine ruled, a sin against nature and, therefore, against God....Celibacy and virginity remained preferred states because they allowed total love of God, 'the spouse of the soul.'"[1]

Augustine would have been pleased with the advent of test-tube babies. In his dilemma over how to reconcile procreation and sex, he wrote: "They who marry wives for this purpose only [procreation], if the means could be given them of having children without intercourse with their wives, would they not with joy unspeakable embrace so great a blessing?"

It is no surprise that historian D. S. Bailey concludes: "Augustine must bear no small measure of responsibility for the insinuation into our culture of the idea still widely current, that Christianity regards sexuality as something peculiarly tainted with evil."

British historian W. E. H. Lecky, in his *History of European Morals,* also observed that marriage was degraded by the early Christians as an inferior state. Although necessary for the propagation of the species, it was considered a necessary evil. But for an individual wanting to maintain the commitment to a Christian life, marriage was more than a compromise; it was nearly a contract of sin. How could one continue to have sex— the "original sin"—*and* aspire to a sin-free life?

St. Bernard used to preach the gospel of marital celibacy so persuasively on street corners in various villages that all the careful wives would hide their husbands when he was in town. Lecky cites various saints who resolved the sexual-marriage–versus–devout-Christian contradiction by leaving their marriages entirely.

The separation between marriage and the priesthood did not begin formally until A.D. 305, when the Spanish Council of Elvira decreed that all married clergy were to abstain from sex with their wives. Up until that time, the clergy married and could maintain sexual lives. So celibate marriage among the clergy was presumably practiced for eight centuries, until the First Lateran Council in A.D. 1123 prohibited marriage for priests. Only toward the end of the thirteenth century was the celibacy of the clergy rigidly enforced.

When Christianity began to branch out into various new sects, the practice of celibacy for the clergy became reserved primarily for Roman Catholicism and Eastern Orthodoxy. And although occasionally recommended, it disappeared almost entirely from the lives of the Protestant clergy. Both John Calvin and Martin Luther upheld the values of celibacy but did not insist on it. As Luther said: "A preacher of the Gospel, if he is able with a good conscience to remain unmarried, let him so remain; but if he cannot abstain, living chastely, then let him take a wife. God has made this plaster for that sore."

As sexuality became more acceptable in Christianity over the centuries, celibacy took on a more rarefied air. Practicing celibates grew further and further apart from the larger society. Celibacy for most Christians continued to be understood as the opposite of sexuality. One was either sexual *or* celibate. And as sexuality became more "natural," celibacy seemed to become more "unnatural." Today, celibacy has become a major issue in the church—praised by the few and maligned by the many.

Modern Monastic Celibacy: Sexual versus Sexless

In an article on being a nun in America, Sister M. Roberta tells the story of her aunt, also a nun, a woman in her sixties.

The aunt was seated on a train across from another woman who kept glaring at her during the ride. Finally, unable to hide her disgust any longer, the woman turned on her and practically shouted, "What's the matter with you girls? Can't you get a man?"[2]

As of 1987, there were approximately 57,000 Catholic priests in the United States, 189,000 nuns, and 14,000 monks in North and Central America, figures said to be on the decrease.[3] This may be due in part to the way that priests, nuns, and monks are treated in our "sexually liberated" society. Their lives are often evaluated as unnatural rather than understood as spiritual, primarily because so little in our society upholds the possibility of growth through spiritualized sexuality. Joseph Wade, a priest who conducted research on modern religious life, concluded that the life of the religious celibate is seen by others as a life of frustration. Those committed to a religious vocation are judged to be "frustrated in their human desires, trapped in a detested form of life... and forced into close, uncongenial contacts."[4]

Whereas celibates throughout the ages have been regarded at least as uplifting examples of the spiritual development of human life, suggesting the possibility of a life directed to more than worldly ends, today religious celibates are no longer given the respect and admiration they received earlier.

As a result, religious devotees may experience undue prejudice against their commitment from the community, based on such concerns as "How can a celibate understand?" And, according to Wade, they may actually be grieved over by their families. Without much support from the rest of society for their chosen life, some modern monastics experience a kind of personal alienation that can be devastating.

Besides societal prejudice, there are other psychological reasons why monastic life has been found to be so difficult today. Priest Paul Conner explains:

> A comparison of pre-modern times with ours reveals that earlier peoples developed more naturally and sta-

bly at home in their human relationships. . . . Their simpler familial and agrarian society favored this, which
explains in large part why many men and women of
those times were able to live contented lives in the monastic setting. In our technological epoch . . . never having sufficient human love as children and adolescents,
they thirst for it as adults. This is, perhaps, an underlying reason why few committed Christians today seem
able to live contentedly within the confines of strict monastic communities.[5]

Similarly, Wade observed an overall lack of understanding of how to deal with sexuality among the monastics he studied, but he found that those from loving homes were better
adjusted to celibacy. Those with affectionate parents had much
less difficulty accepting their own sexuality, and therefore their
celibacy, than did those who came from homes where there
was little affection or sex education. He found that where there
had been a lack of love in the home, by age thirty and over,
a mental change often takes place—an awareness on the part
of the priest that he is not fulfilled in love.

And where there has been a lack of integration and nat-
uralness, priests report feeling the lack of intimacy and may
experience what Wade describes as an emotional coldness. According to Goergen, celibacy may bring loneliness to the monastic life not because of sexual needs but by ignoring the
more basic need for intimacy and closeness to others. So, despite their religious commitment, some priests may not be
ready for celibacy either physiologically or psychologically. The
years of denial may be overwhelming, especially if attention
is constantly going toward sexuality. One often attends with
great interest to that which one thinks one cannot have. So
whereas for some priests celibacy is natural and comfortable,
for others it is not. And when an unnatural celibacy is compounded by a lack of close friendships and little experience
of love, it is no wonder that a priest may choose rather "to
marry than to burn."

This perhaps explains in part why two decades ago, the Ficter survey researching the outlook and opinions of modern Catholic priests reported that two out of three priests wanted to be permitted to marry and favored voluntary over dogmatic celibacy, saying that optional celibacy would be better than enforced celibacy within the Church.

Despite the protest, in the spring of 1979, Pope John Paul II upheld mandatory celibacy for Roman Catholic priests and nuns and reminded them that Jesus referred to the celibate state "as a gift for the Kingdom of Heaven." The Pope pointed out that no one is forced to take celibate vows and that the priests must not give in to the various forms of manipulation that they meet. Most priests today do maintain celibate lives. However, others are attempting to reconcile their sexual with their religious orientations. It is estimated that between 20 and 40 percent of U.S. priests today are homosexual, of whom about half are entirely celibate.[6] Among heterosexual priests, according to a longitudinal study conducted by psychologist Richard Sipe, about 80 percent are celibate, and the other 20 percent actively sexual.

Among the life celibates, there are many priests, nuns, and monks who have confronted and accepted their sexual natures so completely that they are happily and comfortably celibate. A thirty-four-year-old Catholic priest interviewed by the author had this to say about celibacy:

Celibacy is a very simple thing to me. I have learned to deal with sexuality by simply accepting it and not trying to avoid it as a reality of life. I don't think that being celibate means refusing love. I am by nature a friendly and outgoing fellow and I've shared and will continue to share many happy and joyous times with my family and dear friends during my life—I am, after all, Italian. And through these relationships, I feel my love for God deepen immeasurably. But it is God whom I serve above all. I think you will find that those of us who maintain celibacy in the service of God do not exclude love from our lives but rather seek to uphold its value everywhere, in all our interactions with the world.[7]

SECULAR CELIBACY

In Eastern history, religious and secular life have been much more intertwined than in the West; consequently, the polarization of sexuality versus celibacy or marriage versus spiritual life has not occurred with the same intensity as in Western history. In the East, sexuality and celibacy are considered two expressions of the same energy phenomenon.

In general, sex in the East represents the spending of energy, and celibacy its conservation. Excessive sexual interest is not considered a sin but rather a weakness, an unnecessary waste of mental and physical energy, whereas celibacy represents mental and physical strength through the conserving of energy. It is recognized that sex is the basis of celibacy and celibacy the basis of sex. But one has to be sexually ready to be celibate. One accepts one's sexuality, and then, if physiology permits, proceeds to its more refined values in the celibate state.

There are those in the East who have wrongly advocated celibacy as the ideal means of birth control for whole nations, regardless of the sexual and spiritual readiness of individuals to practice it, leading to unfortunate results in overpopulation. But when practiced by those for whom it is sexually timely and useful, celibacy has been generally respected as a means of personal growth throughout the history of Eastern life.

Not so in the West. Here, the practice of celibacy in secular life has had a confused and fragmented history. There have been no large movements to celibate life, nor have any major societies embraced celibacy as a secular spiritual discipline. Rather, at its best, celibacy has been an experiment for certain individuals and communities seeking ways to bring about self-fulfillment and/or social change. At its worst, celi-

bacy has been misused as a means of severe repression to uphold an antisexual position.

In a civilization where sex has been, for the most part, a
heavily charged (mostly negative) issue, celibacy has also been
a charged issue—sometimes revered and sometimes reviled—
based not on its developmental usefulness but on its seemingly antisexual nature. Of course, as psychologist Joe K.
Adams suggests, "There is good reason to believe that the
sex taboos in Western civilization have never prevented or
even minimized the forbidden sexual activities themselves."[8]
And there is also good reason to believe that the practice of
celibacy was never widely accepted beyond its theoretical
virtuousness. Where it had been practiced, celibacy in the
West had often been "unnatural" and caused great suffering;
and where it had been abandoned completely, its loss had
also caused great suffering.

In ancient Greece, celibacy was often actually treated as a
crime. For example, at one time the city of Sparta denied the
rights of citizenship to unmarried men. But around the same
era, in 529 B.C., the mathematician Pythagoras established a
small community at Croton in South Italy to study and practice sexual abstinence and vegetarianism. And, of course, the
most famous secular formulation of celibate love—Platonic
love—was created in this culture in Plato's "ideal society." In
this society, human love transcends its sexual limitations and
becomes a quest for the Ideal of love—an eternal, non-
changing basis for all experiences of fulfillment in love. Love
is considered the basis for union, sex but an unnecessary di-
version. Platonic love is described as a powerful means of coming to experience the unity or wholeness of life, which is far
beyond the sexual. In this way, celibacy allows the self in love
to rise to another plane of reality.

Later on, in the first century A.D., the philosopher Apol-
lonius of Tyana espoused celibate living for his disciples to aid
detachment and equilibrium in thought. Similarly, the Stoics
of the Roman Empire, who replaced the sensual Epicureans,
favored the discipline of celibacy. In A.D. 50, for example, the

Stoic philosopher Epictetus taught that celibacy would calm the philosopher, balance his body and mind, and free him from distracting family cares.

Then there were the famed Vestal Virgins of ancient Rome. During their requisite thirty years of service, celibacy was, of course, maintained, but even after the service was ended, many of the women chose to remain celibate and single throughout the rest of their lives.

During the early days of Christianity, writes Herbert Richardson, in *Nun, Witch, Playmate*, marriage was considered quite unholy because it allowed sexual activity even if only for procreation. Thus, "the commitment to permanent virginity as the basis for a truly spiritual marriage became a not uncommon practice." According to historian D. S. Bailey, this phenomenon of spiritual marriage in secular life was called *syneisaktism* and was "a co-habitation of the sexes under conditions of strict continence, a couple sharing the same house, often the same room, and sometimes even the same bed, yet conducting themselves as brother and sister."

During the Middle Ages and later, it was the laity or secular society who were said to have introduced the concept of spiritualized love between men and women (which included the celibate practices for men discussed in a later chapter). It was called courtly or romantic love and was thought of as the secular attempt to personalize the feelings associated with the love of God.

At that time, the love of God had become a somewhat distant, depersonalized experience, almost completely associated with the church alone. As the churches grew vaster and their spires higher in the seeming attempt to touch God in heaven, the desire to share devotional love with someone on a more intimate, more human scale was structured into the procedures of courtly or romantic love.

According to Herbert Richardson, courtly love extended the sexual process to include a number of "symbolic-affective" steps, each an end in itself. Different steps were taken for different relationships—a romantic conversation, a kiss, or more physical behavior, depending on the situation. It was, no doubt, the forerunner of our "step-by-step" dating procedure, but the steps were not goal-oriented. Rather, they were expressions of the value of a particular relationship. It was, says Richardson, a specific voluntary control over sexual behavior to gain the rewards of intimacy. It ultimately permitted all forms of sexuality "excepting orgasm"—orgasm being involuntary and unintentional and thus considered nonpersonal in expression. As Richardson concludes, "To make sex an expression of love requires a learning process. The courtly lovers abstained, therefore, from all those aspects of sexual interaction that they could not bring within the range of personal intention and voluntary control."

Courtly love eventually lost its appeal. Later on, when the love relationships between men and women were commonly accepted as primarily physical, the regulations of courtly love were laughed at as restrictive and unnatural. Shakespeare, the Romantics, and Freud were among its critics. But only seeing it as sexually repressive, they failed to recognize how freely it allowed love to grow.

Courtly love, perhaps *because* of its conscious rules, ennobled the ideal of love in very personal human relationships, yet it never allowed the lovers to become overshadowed in their expression of love. It was never false or overblown: devotional love grew in accordance with the consciousness of the lovers who maintained full awareness of every act and chose each act of love for the accuracy of its expression. What it lacked in spontaneity it made up for in clarity. It was not confusing or disorderly; it allowed for balanced growth of all parts of the personality in the cause of loving. Moreover, it stands as perhaps the best example in Western history of the use of celibacy in the service of growth through love.

Throughout the centuries to come, as sexuality became negatively repressed instead of positively controlled, the "sinful" character of sex would often so dominate human relations that personal love too would become degraded and no longer regarded as an appropriate channel for the development of human life. We can speculate that this is where celibacy got the bad reputation it has today, when it became falsely associated with sexual repression rather than with the growth of love.

This situation came about many times in Western history—as sin and sex were many times confused. As Barbara Tuchman insightfully remarked, "Of all mankind's ideas, the equating of sex with sin has left the greatest train of trouble." And if, as Donald Goergen observed, we identify sexual desire as sinful, "repression is almost inevitable." And a time of sexual repression was never more clearly in evidence in Western history than in America.

The Puritans

Starting with the Puritans, America began its amazing history of sexual repression. In the seventeenth century, the Puritans used religion as the watchdog of sexual activity, and Christianity continued its history of what one scholar calls "sex-centered ideology."

The dour *New England Primer* opened with the famous couplet:

> *In Adam's Fall*
> *We sinned all.*

So as the Puritan child began to read, starting with the first letter of the alphabet, the first concept he or she learned was that of original sin. Yet there was no secrecy about sex for the Puritans. They were realists, says historian Milton Rugoff, "only too well-aware of the hungers of the body." They had no faith in voluntary celibacy but believed that sexual desires—"the most subversive of total devotion to God"—could only be suppressed by fear-induced continence based on wrath and denunciation. They didn't deny sexuality shyly, they denounced it vociferously.

But by the nineteenth century, sexuality had become so repressed as to be almost invisible. No longer a hellfire-and-damnation religious issue, it had become an internalized conflict—a psychological and moral issue and a breeding ground for our modern rebellion.

America was the land of freedom and expansion in almost every area except the sexual. Even while Americans were settling a continent and constantly experimenting with new methods and innovative solutions, sexuality was taboo, considered totally shameful, and narrow rules for sex were rigidly adhered to. But, says Rugoff, there is "a law of sexual dynamics: repression eventually breeds evasion or rebellion." And both these reactions occurred in America's sexual history.

Lacking any real knowledge of the realities of sexuality, nineteenth-century Americans focused heavily upon its mysteries and progressed in a peculiarly American way in two different sexual directions—some toward further self-denial, which became "quiet evasion" in the conforming lives of the Victorians, and some toward an increased freedom of sexual expression in the experimental communities of the latter part of the century. Celibacy was prescribed in both cases—but in one its use was wholly negative and in the other quite sophisticated and positive.

The Victorians

Whereas the Puritans had waged great, loud battles to suppress sexuality, the Victorians were so horrified by sex that they completely denied its existence. The Victorian ideal was the total sublimation of sex—"nothing showing." It wasn't discussed, but it was certainly implied. The outer appearances of propriety were valued far more than any hidden realities. But under the surface of respectability, prostitution and unsafe abortion were practiced everywhere.

In family life, sexual love was seen as degrading—"for the beasts only." Men were acknowledged to have sexual desires but were supposed to refrain from imposing them on their wives. They tried cold showers, exercise, hard beds, religious prayer, and eventually, prostitutes. The concept of propriety in marriage overtook all normal feelings of love and became an intense kind of prudery, not a striving for purity. Wives, however, were not even supposed to have sexual desires at all and were taught to participate in procreative sexual activity only for the benefit of their spouses and families. Thus they led virtually celibate lives. (Not that any aspect of women's physical makeup could have been known: the prudery of the times was so great that female cadavers could not even be dissected in the medical schools.)

But the Victorians' attempt to eradicate their sexuality was to no avail. By attempting to negate eroticism, everything became eroticized. A glance, an uncovered ankle, a blushing cheek all took on special sexual significance in the absence of other possibilities. So the time and energy spent in the interior lives of the Victorians on sexualized thinking—not only in America, but in England and the "more civilized" parts of Europe as well—turned out to be much greater than in many less repressive eras.*

Not until the beginning of this century did a lifting of these self-imposed sexual sanctions begin to occur, partly under the mutually reinforcing influences of the advent of birth control and the public awareness of the theories of Freud and his contemporaries. Central to the new thinking on sexuality was the

---

*Despite the influence of Freud, not every authority considers the sexual restrictiveness of the nineteenth century to be entirely negative. At least one eminent historian, Arnold Toynbee, concludes that the denial of sexuality represented the overcoming of biological boundaries and became an important contributing factor in the century's great creative expansion. He wrote: "I admire the nineteenth century West's success in postponing the age of sexual awakening, sexual experience and sexual infatuation far beyond the age of physical puberty. You may tell me that this was against nature; but to be human consists precisely in transcending nature—in overcoming the biological limitations that we have inherited from our pre-human ancestors." ("Why I Dislike Western Civilization," *New York Times Magazine*, May 10, 1964.)

idea that sexuality is neither criminal, nor sinful, nor abnormal.

And eventually, relatively "sin-free" sex began to take on the aura of actual enjoyment, even though it was "enjoyed" very seriously. The experts of the day began to "prescribe" it, following Freud's admonition that sexual repression caused neuroses and untold physical ailments. Then came the theory that celibacy was actually harmful because the reproductive organs would grow weak if not used regularly. This idea was then soundly protested by such physicians as Dr. Arthur Gould, who argued in 1906, "If that were true, the boy who exercises his sexuality regularly from youth onward should have the greatest sexual strength—but the reverse is true. Sexual power is never lost through abstinence, as the ability to weep is not lost through not weeping."

According to Gould, semen that is not secreted is redistributed throughout the body to nourish brain, muscles, bones, and sinews. He considered "spermatazoa the most highly vitalized form of living matter... the most precious nutriment of the blood.... Overproduction of semen from either thought or practice is a serious strain and waste of vitality."

The idea of sexual waste of valuable energy and youth was a direct steal from the East but was echoed by a number of Westerners in the first decades of this century. And Bertrand Russell and others concluded that not only were the physical strains of sex excessive, but the mental and social attention put on things sexual also were excessive and, ultimately, dangerous.

At the same time that Victorian America was furtively covering and uncovering ankles, a small group of Americans began to seek new ways to live together, free of self-deception and pretension. Thus, in the mid-nineteenth century, a number of structured communities were founded to promote a social concept or purpose for ideal community life. These communities attracted what Rugoff calls the "spiritual avant-garde of the period"—young people who were seeking ways to satisfy their spiritual longings and "Puritan monks, who rejected the world and saw celibacy and labor as a loftier, more spiritual way of life."

Among these societies were those experimenting in "free love," but, interestingly, some form of celibacy often formed the basis for the sexual freedom. And other experimental communities were exclusively celibate.

Herbert Richardson compares these American utopian societies of the nineteenth century with the monastic traditions which emerged during medieval times—wherein the communities, by "renouncing sexual intercourse and raising celibacy to an ideal," were reorienting sexual desire to a new form of expression—the spiritual "communalization" of sex.

The Utopians

The most famous of the secular American celibates were (and still are) the Shakers. The Shaker community, founded near Albany, New York, was a close-knit society of men and women which was aimed at "perfect simplicity." The words of their well-known song perhaps best illustrate their outlook:

> *Tis the gift to be simple—*
> *Tis the gift to be free—*
> *Tis the gift to come down where we ought to be.*
> *And when we find ourselves in the place just right—*
> *Twill be in the valley of love and delight.*
> *When true simplicity is gained,*
> *To bow and to bend—we shan't be ashamed.*
> *To turn and to turn*
> *Will be our delight*
> *'Till by turning, turning, we come round right.*

The "turning" no doubt refers, at least in part, to the ritual "dance" that the Shakers performed. Most interpreters of this "whirling" activity see it as a technique the Shakers used to "neutralize the desire for coition" or as a release of sexual tension. The "dance" is also often considered to be orgasmic—a form of communal sex growing from the renunciation of genital sex and leading to what Richardson calls "a new polymorphous total sexuality." But there are also other dimensions of the "turning-around" ritual to consider.

When one whirls around continuously, the outer external cues one generally relies upon for locating oneself in space tend to disappear and one may experience a moment of unboundedness, free of outward boundaries. So this Shaker ritual can also be understood as a technique for freeing oneself from physical limitations, if only temporarily—where reliance on inner cues is called for—in order to "come round right." One thus becomes momentarily self-reliant, free from the field of external information.

The Shaker "dance" may also be deeply symbolic and spiritual in intent and effect: a way to "shake off" pride, egotism, shame, or any of the human weaknesses that disallow the experience of "true simplicity" and deep humility—the simplest form of the self, free from all personality restrictions—"'Till by turning, turning, we come round right."

The Shakers led the exemplary life of pure monasticism. All arose and retired at the same time: everyone dined together in silence. No stimulants such as coffee, tea, alcohol, or tobacco were permitted, and disease was considered a "sin against God." The Shakers understood God to have both male and female characteristics and saw the purpose of union to be union *within* the individual, not just union between two individuals. So remaining celibate for them was a way to be like God.

Despite, or perhaps because of, their impressive self-discipline, the Shakers were observed to be warm and affectionate with each other. Although men and women were not allowed to talk together privately, all shared a common purpose and a common communication possibly reaching far deeper than words. All maintained celibacy, even the married couples who joined.

The communal efforts of the Shakers in material production were very successful; they structured an environment of purposefulness and creativity and became well known as great inventors and innovators. (One familiar area of Shaker design—furniture making—produced some of the most beautiful pieces ever made in America.) Yet, even at their peak of productivity, in 1860, there were only 6000 members. Since no children are born in the community, membership is only maintained if new people join. By 1900 the membership had decreased to 1000, and today there are only a few. (During the 1960s, some members of the counterculture tried to join the Shaker community but did not last long, apparently unable to keep up with the disciplined pace of Shaker life.)

Other celibate communities of nineteenth-century America included the Rappites of New Harmony, Indiana, and (later) Economy, Pennsylvania. The 800-member society was founded by a German industrialist less for the purpose of spiritual living than for economic reasons. The Rappites were willing to forego sex in order to secure freedom from financial want. Like the Shakers, their work productivity was enormous and of the highest quality, and they grew to be a very wealthy community. All were celibate, but in the interests of maintaining economic growth, married couples were allowed to live together for procreative purposes one year out of seven.

Another midcentury community was the Memnonia Society, founded in Yellow Springs, Ohio. This was a community advancing not work productivity but the social experiment of "free love." Its small membership paid to join, much as one would at a vacation resort or health spa. A ninety-day celibacy was required before sexual union between any of the members was allowed. This was structured in order for the experience of sexual union to be given time to grow in the qualities of spiritual union as well. Besides celibacy, certain Eastern techniques of lovemaking were practiced along with vegetarianism and water fasts—all activities geared to creating more heightened experiences in the "experiment" of loving.

In 1872, the Oneida Colony—the most bold and successful of all the nineteenth-century experimental communities—

was founded by John Noyes in Oneida, New York. It lasted thirty years and drew hundreds of participants. It too was a love-oriented rather than work-oriented communal experiment. Although not a celibate community, the Oneida Colony is classified with the others because of its commitment to exploration beyond the sexual level of love. The emphasis was on self-control and mental enjoyment of love between members and no one participated in indiscriminate sexuality. Noyes contended that his teachings on sexual practice had more in common with Shaker celibacy than with rampant free sexuality. The participants were given techniques to develop the heart and the spiritual possibilities of love. Under these circumstances, even multiple marriages were permitted.

The members of the Oneida community were taught by Noyes to distinguish between the "amative" and the "procreative" functions in lovemaking and to determine when each should be used according to its correct need. In amative love, male ejaculation was prohibited, in order, said Noyes, to make possible "the highest bliss of sexual fellowship for any length of time." Oneida became well known for the practice of this technique of male continence, which was used to teach maximum self-control as well as to allow the prolonged enjoyment of what Noyes described as "the sweetest and noblest period of intercourse... that first moment of simple presence and spiritual effusion before the muscular exercise begins." But the male also learned not to ejaculate because Noyes considered it "a wasteful expenditure of the seed and, therefore, unnatural."

Noyes advocated the same technique that Roman Catholics call *coitus reservatus* and that the Indian Tantric texts recommend for optimal male pleasure. (It is also known as *karezza* from the Italian for "caress.") Researcher Shere Hite refers to the revival of this technique today by experimenting male groups. Alfred C. Kinsey described its results as follows:

> In this technique it is common for the individual to experience as many as a dozen or twenty peaks of response which, while closely approaching the sexual

climax, deliberately avoid what we should interpret as actual orgasm. Persons who practice such techniques commonly insist that they experience orgasm at each and every peak even though each is held to something below full response and...ejaculation is avoided.[9]

This technique was practiced at Oneida until children were desired and then the procreative function was employed.

In all these communities, whether truly celibate or not, the control or refinement of sexuality in a knowledgeable and positive way obviously distinguished them from the larger society where sex continued to be thought of as bad and worthy of revulsion only. In none of the small societies, not even among the Shakers, was sexuality degraded; it was merely unattended to in the face of other goals considered more important for the community. Like the Eastern cultures which served at times as the models for these nineteenth-century communal enterprises, celibacy was a discipline for the purpose of human development, not for the purpose of ridding oneself of sexuality.

Modern Celibacy in Community: The Joy of Sects

In his book on new monastic communities, Charles Fracchia describes a growing trend toward monastic life in the United States paralleling the recent religious reawakening. The new monastics are emerging from the fifty million unmarried adults in this country, all searching, says Fracchia, for a life in a community. These spiritual enterprises are springing up not only in the deserts and mountains but also in the middle of large cities.

The emphasis, while definitely spiritual, is also familial— the sense of being part of a family is equally as important as the religious rites practiced. Living with this mutual support, the new community participants say they can more easily live a religious life free from some of its harsher realities such as loneliness and economic deprivation, often made more harsh in modern times.

Some of these communities are following in the footsteps of the Shakers and the other nineteenth-century work communities and have developed very successful cottage industries in order to be self-sufficient and independent from the larger society. They bake bread, preserve fruits, sell weaving, pottery, and other commercial products. They work not only for economic purposes but "to experience God in the simplest tasks of daily living."

All faiths are represented in these communities but not necessarily along the old religious lines. For example, many Jewish and Catholic men and women were found to be participating in the Eastern spiritual communities—some even becoming priests and nuns within their new orders—and a number of non-Christians are turning toward the new Christianity. But the emphasis is often on regaining the "true" nature of the religious enterprise as formulated not 20 years ago but 2000 years ago, when the focus was on the idea of community in religious life.

The spiritual commitment of the new monastics is to personal growth, not simply to the dogmatized or ritualized aspects of religion. In this way, no real distinctions between the priest and the lay person are upheld—the common bonds of spiritual life are what bring these people together.

While the official church worries about the indifference of the laity, these young people are embracing monastic lifestyles that adhere to an even more rigorous morality than the church itself advocates. And in these societies, celibacy is often mandatory or at least desirable. The members learn to love each other "in community," as helpmates but not sexual mates.

One such community is Weston Priory in Vermont, where 700 to 1000 city people come on weekends to participate in the spiritual life of the monastery. Like the Shakers, the monks of Weston Priory use dance to celebrate prayer and worship.

Then there are the Eastern communities such as the Buddhist Orthodox group in northern California where men and women live separately and celibately. There are also modern

Christian groups, such as the Holy Order of MANS—a non-denominational mystic organization that requires celibacy for its membership even during the year preceding the formal commitment.

At a solar-heated Benedictine monastery in New Mexico, single men and women—both secular and religious—live together but are celibate. One monk living there described the community: "We've all found that the importance of interaction between men and women in this community—and, mind you, we are all vowed to celibacy, even those who are in temporary commitment... is of inestimable value. The men and women complement each other."

The members are each assigned a "prayer partner" of the opposite sex. "We become very close to each other—like brother and sister—sharing each other's thoughts and feelings, ministering to each other. We are celibate, but we love one another. You know, I think this is a great preparation for marriage."

One nun comments on her experience:

> I lived in a community of women for more than twenty years, and I must honestly say that I far prefer a mixed community.... My own experience and that of people in the community here attest to the fact that you can have a celibate community composed of both men and women. Also, certain negative aspects of communities, either of all men or all women are lessened in a mixed community. The women become less petty and the men become softer.[10]

These new communities are essentially looking to establish a revival of spiritual life integrated with personal development. Celibacy offers the participants a new and perhaps deeper look at love. The "spiritualization" of life is based on the understanding and experience of the growth of nonsexual love—a concept that will be examined in the next chapter.

Celibacy and Love

Does abstinence make the heart grow fonder?

LOVE LESSONS

3 As our society moves into a more careful yet possibly more expansive era of relationships, we are faced with the need to learn some new lessons about love. In our modern society until now, young people have been clearly taught that learning to have sex is a more important accomplishment than learning to love.

As the more subtle feelings of love became dominated by the more valued feelings of sexuality, eventually the love response became more difficult to stimulate—especially apart from the sexual response. Many therapists are finding that a growing number of the people they treat have to relearn how to love independently from sex. Essentially, they have to be instructed in what love comprises without constant reliance on accompanying sexual desires.

We've all been well taught that sexual attraction can be experienced separate from love—but somehow we've been coerced into believing that love apart from sex doesn't exist or, if it does exist, it doesn't mean much. We forget that in most relationships, the sexual aspect is neither the most important nor the most common ground for relating. One can relate nonsexually to everyone. We relate sexually only to a very few. And if a person finds that he or she must relate sexually to everyone, it is usually due to a pathological distortion of the personality. It is likely that, by trying to meet the need for love primarily through sexual activity, some people in our society have been "educated" or have trained themselves to exclude all other feelings of love in favor of the sexual ones. And this training may be starting at an early age.

Learning to Touch

Up until now, children have been observed to be most open to nonsexual loving because habits to express love sexually have not yet been fully ritualized in them. In an essay on love, Joe Adams notes that children are able to love far more often and more easily than adults. He concludes that in terms of availability of impulses and feelings, "the average middle-aged person is quite dead" when compared with a healthy lively child. He explains that this happens because when an impulse or feeling cannot be expressed appropriately it will "gradually disappear or be transformed in some other impulse or feeling."[1]

But children today often try to be sexual in adult ways before their bodies are ready to be so. Once they learn how to "act" sexual, they behave sexually more by mimicking what they have learned from the adult culture than by playing in a genuinely childlike sexual way. In the push to educate children in sexual matters, education in matters of loving is all but ignored. It is strange to consider that in the endless controversy over sex education in the schools, the issue hardly ever arises whether sex is even an appropriate thing to teach apart from an education in love. If children were taught all the ways there are to love, then sex would be taught as one possible way to express this most basic human need.

Children learn to love by being loved from birth on. It is as essential as food. No one has ever died from a lack of sex, no matter how unfortunate they may feel, but research on infant needs conducted by René Spitz, Harry Harlow, John

Bowlby, and others has demonstrated that without love, expressed in physical tenderness and cuddling, infant mortality rates go up significantly. And while not literally a cause of death for most adults, the lack of loving can create tremendous loneliness and even illness.

One of the major symptoms of our national avoidance of love and the nonsexual expression of feelings is the unwillingness to be physically close to and actually touch other people. Such avoidance would be understandable in a culture where sex was very much repressed, but in our culture it is often considered more inappropriate to touch others nonsexually than to have sex with them! This is because we generally don't touch other people *unless* we are going to have sex with them. This taboo on "interpersonal tactility," on touching—is, says Ashley Montagu, at least as great as the sexual taboo has been through the ages, both having arisen, he surmises, from Christianity. But where we seem to have overcome the sexual taboo, we have not yet overcome the touch taboo.

As a matter of fact, we Americans are notorious for having created a "no-touch" culture. Sex is one of the only ways we allow ourselves to touch and be touched. Often the desire to be touched gets confused with the desire to have sex, when all one really wants is a little body contact of the mildest sort.

As a result, human behavior experts have found that while touching is one of the most basic indications of love and lack of hostility, many people are deprived of the touch experience—both giving and receiving—to such an extent that they do not learn how to express emotion through touch. This deprivation is said to extend from childhood on and, not surprisingly, is found to be a specific problem related to sexual dysfunction. At their Research Institute in St. Louis, sex researchers Masters and Johnson have spent a great deal of their therapeutic time teaching their dysfunctional patients how to express themselves simply through touching by a technique they call "sensate focusing." By teaching clients to focus on the sense of touch and on all the senses, Masters and

Johnson use this more basic human response to help develop the sexual response. This has been found to be the right procedure to retrace the developmental behavioral sequence of learned inhibition from as early a stage as infancy where the baby and later the child learns "not to touch."

Masters and Johnson and other sex therapists may see the more extreme cases where fear of touching has contributed to the socially more disturbing phenomenon of sexual dysfunction. But there are many people who can function well sexually and still not touch. This is the symptom not of sexual dysfunction but of "intimacy dysfunction."

The Growth to Intimacy

Intimacy is one of the most desired yet one of the most threatening of human experiences. It may be difficult for us to be intimate, but it is, after all, the intimacy that we long for in relationships, the intimacy that we value above all else. Rollo May pinpoints this longing when he writes that in remembering sexual experiences, it is the intimacy that is remembered, not the orgasm.

According to most psychologists, the reason we are afraid of being intimate, of allowing another person to get close to us emotionally, is because most of us are concerned that when our loved ones see us as we "really are," they will discover how shallow and inadequate we are "underneath." And so, the repudiation of intimacy is said to be based on feelings of unworthiness and a lack of confidence in oneself. To preserve a vivid love experience, one may feel compelled to push the lover away in order to avoid any resulting depreciation, rebuffs, frustration, dependency, or any other experience that one feels may burst the bubble of love for good.

Of course no one likes to be overshadowed by another or to feel that he or she will be judged inadequate. The fear of losing oneself in the relationship is a very valid fear. But such a fear will never be overcome unless one allows oneself to experience the depths of one's own feelings. Until a person knows on her own through her own understanding of herself that she is a truly worthy person, no one else can convince her of that worthiness. Many can try, but always there will be that self-doubt, the fear of being discovered as a sham, that will continue to inhibit the willingness to grow in any relationship. When this growth is disallowed, a lack of intimacy develops, and the result is loneliness—even within a longtime marriage.

Many psychologists and psychotherapists, including Harry Stack Sullivan, Erik Erikson, Abraham Maslow, and Carl Jung distinguish carefully between sexual activity and the need for intimacy. As Rollo May has said, "For human beings, the more powerful need is not for sex *per se* but for relationships, intimacy, acceptance and affirmation."

Sex is, in fact, often used as an excuse for actually avoiding intimacy. If one is afraid of the surrender required for growing intimacy, sex can be used as a cover for that fear. So at its worst, sexual exchange is judged on how well one has *avoided* getting close during the experience: "Wow, I was somewhere else that time!"

But at the same time that sex may be used as an escape from the threat of intimacy, it is also the *only* way many people know *to* be intimate. So what may happen is that the deep yearnings of two people to grow closer are frustrated by this one limited choice of love communication on which they depend for fulfillment and growth of intimacy. Every time we long for union but find that of course we are still two after orgasm, there is a sense of failure. It is not the fault of the sex act but of one's misplaced desires and expectations. Taken by itself, sex becomes an unfortunate and inappropriate catchall for all the human love needs.

Masters and Johnson also recognized this deeper need for intimate love that goes beyond sexuality. In *The Pleasure Bond* they wrote: "Intimacy must be nourished by a mutuality between a man and a woman that may include, but must go beyond, the physical fact of intercourse. Intimacy, like any other emotion, must either grow and become deeper or it must wither and die.... Neither physical interchange nor physical intimacy is a sound basis for a continuing relationship."[2]

When nonsexual intimacy does grow and deepen in relationships, its growth is generally based not on wild, passionate feelings but on inner stability and security—on the deepening experience of individual personal happiness and contentment that is then shared in the relationship. Many people report that they enjoy this slowly growing kind of intimacy more than the back-and-forth instability of passion in their romantic involvements. In her study of romance, Elaine Walster concluded that at least half her subjects preferred the companion-type love of affection and deep friendship to the vagaries of "wild romance."

The intimacy of deep friendship can occur along with sexual intimacy, but sexual activity is not necessary for its growth. When this kind of intimacy does occur along with sexual expression, the experience of sexuality has been found to be very different from the overshadowing kind of sexuality that can literally take one's breath away. (During those times of "heavy breathing," we may be trying to keep our attention and feelings centered on the subtleties of sharing love, but often we're barely able to pick up the refinements in the experience because of blocked air passages caused by swollen blood vessels—a heart pumping very rapidly; we're trying to maintain heightened consciousness when everything physiological is conspiring to reduce our awareness and cut us off from the experience!)

When sex is stabilized in intimacy, another kind of experience happens. It is one of expansion, delicacy, fullness. This tender kind of sexual love is universally described as serene, nonthreatening, and comforting.

But it's not the sexual experience which brings about that serenity. One must be *already* stable and secure within oneself if one wishes to have the way opened for such intimacy to occur while maintaining sexual activity. In other words, happiness is the requirement for enjoyable sex; sex is not the basis for happiness.

Sexual love is just one kind of love. Most love relationships are celibate. Celibate love is love that could be sexual but isn't. It's true that all love has the potential to be expressed sexually, but not all love is *best* expressed sexually. Thus only a few relationships are sexual. And since celibate relationships are far more common than sexual ones, we are far more experienced in how to be celibate than in how to be sexual. Most of us have experienced how a relationship changes when it shifts from a sexual to a celibate status or vice versa. Oftentimes people may feel more comfortable and more loving in the Platonic relationships than in the more overshadowing complexities of the sexual ones. This is not because those relationships are "better": it is really because love is less likely to be restricted in its nonsexual expression than in a love relationship focused on that one overriding concern—which often occurs when sexuality dominates the relationship. Since sex tends to bring a lot of expectations with it, people tend to be more demanding in sexual affairs than in nonsexual ones. And they tend to be more disappointed in sexual relationships—due to higher expectations perhaps, but also to higher restrictions on the outcome of time spent together. Sexual relating seems to be less open-ended, less multifaceted, if only because sexual attention is often trained to be drawn to the goal of activity rather than to the activity itself.

Celibacy can help to break that pattern of training and limitation in love relations by removing the focus on sex in order to further explore love without the boundaries. By drawing one's love energy away from genital expression, a new range of expression is opened. Released from the one field of sexual activity, love is spontaneously transformed into a more subtle flow of energy, perhaps best thought of as a "frictionless flow"—love unimpeded by any action or by any boundary.

This flow is what celibate married couples report that they particularly enjoy: a kind of surrender in love in which feelings of tenderness grow deeper—an increasingly deeper contact. One couple described it as "a subtle but permanent orgasm, not offset by fatigue or boredom." It is love that grows automatically but does not need to be acted upon, generously available at all times. This full feeling of love is an essential part of human development and various descriptions have been put forth to explain it.

KINDS OF LOVE

The experience of love and loving changes throughout life. As one grows out of one kind of love, one becomes absorbed in the next. But one rarely learns how to integrate the easy intimacy of trust and sharing learned in nonsexual ways with the Big Adult Sexual Relationship. Often we only consider an adult relationship to be a "real" one *if* it is sexual. We forget the value of all the nonsexual relationships and the high quality of love they engender—in the quest to secure what has been designated the "best" kind of love.

Surveying the field of love from the celibate vantage point, a certain balance is gained when one realizes the extent of possibilities for real intimacy to open the heart in love—in which sexual expression is just one opportunity, and not necessarily the best one at all times.

The Primary Love Relationship: Self-Love

> The love for my own self is inseparably connected with
> the love for any other being.
>
> ——ERICH FROMM

It is well known that the love one feels for oneself is indispensable in one's ability to love others. We learn to love ourselves through the experiences of being loved—through parents, teachers, friends, and so on. It is the way to discover one's own inner strengths and values—the secret unchanging nature of one's central being. And then we learn to love ourselves *in* others—through the opportunities they give us to love them. This basic kind of love is presexual. As psychiatrist Peter Koestenbaum describes it, "It is a transaction between one pure inward consciousness and another. The physical accoutrements are incidental, later, separate... [this] love is an encounter of awareness... [it] is thus closer to deep friendship than to sexual relations."[3]

Some evaluate self-love as the only kind of love that truly exists because it is the key ingredient in all the experiences of love one has throughout life. And the love one feels even as it extends outward is still love of oneself—you can only love anything as it expresses *you.*

So it is that self-love has many dimensions, each of which pertains to different relationships structured in different levels of consciousness or self-awareness. Many kinds of love are really simply further extensions of self-love produced by increased awareness of one's sphere of loving. Whether it is another individual, a family group, or a society to which we belong and with whom we share a common purpose—social, political, religious, scientific, artistic—whether a business, a baseball team, a nation, all the emotions and loyalties that elicit the response "LOVE" in the heart are extensions of how one feels about oneself.

Or we love ourselves in nature—seeing nature not as something *apart from* ourselves, but as a part *of* ourselves. It inspires our development; for example, we love nature as it inspires us to represent it in creations of our own—music, art, and the like—or as we create conditions to uncover its hidden mysteries in scientific laboratories or through personal exploration of its mountains and seas.

All aspects of such relationships that one has with the world are founded in the self—and certain qualities of the self grow in relation to certain experiences provided for us by nature. These are the qualities of love found in all particular relationships.

Self-Actualized Love

One of the most prominent authorities on love in recent years was the psychologist Abraham Maslow. In his studies on self-actualized people—people who were living more of their full potential in life—Maslow was able to delineate some of the ideal qualities of love.

The primary quality he found was self-sufficiency. According to his observations, self-sufficiency is the basis for love in the successful relationships of self-actualized people:

> Self-actualizing people don't *need* each other as do ordinary lovers. They can be extremely close yet go apart quite easily.... Throughout the most intense and ecstatic love affairs, these people remain themselves and remain ultimately masters of themselves as well, living by their own standards even though enjoying each other intensely.... The ego is in one sense merged with another, but yet in another sense remains separate and strong as always.

Another quality of love Maslow found to be distinguishable in self-actualized people is spontaneity: "They love because they are loving persons, in the same way that they are kind, honest, natural, i.e., because it is their nature to be so spontaneously, as a strong man is strong without willing to be, as a rose emits perfume or as a child is childish."[4]

Maslow further described love as fullness, as a quality of life which reflects fullness in waves of joy which emanate automatically from a person full of love.

Another value of love which Maslow brings to our attention is its nonpossessiveness. This quality lets love grow between people toward a kind of freedom that enables both to remain fully themselves deep within the shared experience. "In the same way," he wrote, "we can enjoy a painting without wanting to own it, a rosebush without wanting to pluck from it, a pretty baby without wanting to kidnap it...so also can one person admire and enjoy another in a non-doing or non-getting way."

Maslow's descriptions of qualities of love find support in the observations of many others. One well-known authority on love was the philosopher Martin Buber, who defined love as the totality of one's self coming face to face with the totality of another in what he called the "I-Thou" relationship. According to Buber, the love between the two is unrestricted; it is essentially "cosmic," entirely natural, in that nature regulates it perfectly—therefore it is spontaneous, self-sufficient, always full, and certainly nonpossessive. It is likened to the air we breathe—always there generously for us to partake of it fully. And it requires another general quality of ideal love: unconditionality.

Unconditional Love: Mother Love

A mother's love is often described as the best example of unconditional love. How the mother behaves toward her child when she herself feels happy and secure is on the basis of never-ending love. Without any struggle or effort on her part, she provides a source of constant fullness of love. She loves her child solely because it is her child. Mother's love is basically *uncontrived*, not learned or controlled. As Erich Fromm has described it, its presence "gives the loved person a sense of bliss."

It is this maternal love, the love expressed in tenderness, respect, and care that Ashley Montagu says is the "love that should and can exist between male and female" in its developed form. It is the ideal of devotional love, made all the more full when experienced by two adults who share its unconditional nurturance. Through mother's love, the child is taught to love himself or herself; through the sweetness of that love, the adult communicates his or her most intimate feelings of loving to a child and also to those precious adult friends who elicit that tender response.

Admiration, Surrender, and Devotion: The Student/Teacher Relationship

In Eastern cultures in particular, the love for the teacher, the master, or the guide is considered perhaps the most important love relationship in life. Whether one comes upon a teacher by chance or by choice, the necessary ingredient for benefiting maximally from the relationship is said to be love. In the West too, many have experienced something of this kind of love for a grandparent or for a particular teacher in school or elsewhere who seems to have guided much of one's personal destiny and to whom one remains grateful throughout life. It is the love Beethoven is said to have felt for his teacher Carl Czerny or the love Socrates was said to have elicited from his pupils.

The specific qualities of the student love of teacher are most commonly respect, admiration, devotion, and surrender. These qualities allow the student or disciple to become wholly appreciative and therefore wholly receptive to the knowledge that the teacher offers. Based on the openness of the heart, the student responds with more or less openness to the teacher and, when "in love" with the teacher, is able to listen more alertly, think more attentively, and absorb the knowledge more easily.

The love represented in this relationship is the real growth of self-love which the teacher is able to facilitate by opening up a deeper part of the student's self-appreciation. The student experiences a more developed mind and a more loving heart through his devoted admiration for his "idol," thereby taking in the very qualities he loves and admires in the other. He is "pulled," as it were, "up" to his own high standards in himself through his willingness to value their expression in his teacher.

Celibate Passion: Romantic Love

Romantic love has a long history of exploration dating from the courtly love tradition of the Middle Ages. Later developments include its flowering in the Renaissance and the romantic era. Even today, it certainly has not lost much of its appeal.

In a real sense, romantic love "specializes" in celibacy. It can include sexual expression but, more typically, sexuality is the nonactive spur to the intensity of emotion which characterizes it. Since sexual relating is not the purpose or the means for establishing the relationship, the requirements of celibacy serve to free the love and the lover from what Bertrand Russell calls "all sexual alloy." Celibacy thus serves to energize the ecstasy and intense delight.

Romantic love has the distinction of being regarded as the most passionate kind of love shared between people. Its qualities are intensity, devotion, and purposeful aspiration. It is said to be based on a mysterious attraction that draws two people inevitably together: the more abstract and subtle the attraction remains, the more powerful it feels. Romantic love may occur when "some enchanted evening," you see a stranger across a crowded room looking questioningly at you. But just as quickly the romance can fade when the stranger then asks you where the bathroom is.

Romantic love is really actualized in the lover's quest for the precious object of love. As the desire grows, one's heart becomes more and more full. For romantic love to achieve heights of passion, the love object may have to be difficult to attain for one reason or another—a social barrier or some other form of resistance. This is necessary because the less concrete the relationship, the better. Thus unrequited love is usually very romantic—the love object never falls from perfection because all the object of one's affection has to do is simply exist and serve as a channel for the full expression of one's own nature, as Beatrice was for Dante.

But because it is in a sense a closed system of energy between two people meant to create a high level of concentrated feeling between the two, romantic love seems to require a way to expand in order to maintain the intensity of feeling. Otherwise, romantic love tends to exhaust itself, particularly as the continuation of "the feeling" is often more valued than the commitment to the person. This is perhaps why many believe that romantic love is not a good basis on which to marry, for the feeling could easily subside and turn into disappointment.

Platonic Love: Seeking the Ideal

Perhaps the most famous nonsexual kind of love is what we have come to call Platonic—the nonsexual intimate love between close friends. Often today Platonic love is considered less valuable than sexual love, but in Plato's day it was considered far more valuable. Sexual fulfillment, the waves of emotion so dear to the sexual lover were, for Plato, "the releasing of individual tension rather than an actual merging." But Platonic love also differs from celibate romantic love. Whereas romantic lovers are content to exchange the full measure of their feelings with each other, Platonic lovers yearn for "something bigger than both of us."

Each of us has known someone in whom we see only "the good." No matter what others may tell us or what we try to analyze intellectually, when we are with that person we see radiance and beauty. And with such a person, we feel happy and uplifted. Having experienced this feeling in one person's presence, we long to find it in another. As we search for it, what we are really seeking (says Plato) is the *ideal* of beauty and goodness that would make us feel most fulfilled as human beings. If we are seeking something that falls short of the ideal, we will never be satisfied. To find out what one really is looking for, Plato recommends moral teaching, a scientific education, and some form of spiritual discipline. Through self-knowledge, one learns the purpose of loving, to find the hidden values of life which bring permanent joy. This is the goal of Platonic love.

Spiritual Love

Spiritual love is really the foundation for all other kinds of love. At the same time as it is the culmination of human love (as one experiences the "divine" in others), it is also the source of all the manifestations of love. It incorporates all the qualities of love—respect, tenderness, inspiration, self-sufficiency —and all the kinds of love relationships within its sphere and gives them the maximum chance for development. It is spiritual love which has been found to be the most unbounded, the most freeing, the most elevating, and the most developed kind of love humanly possible.

Spiritual love has been recognized throughout the ages as the ideal vehicle for seeking perfection in life. It has been declared the means by which we transcend the limits of "ordinary" love to discover a deeper aspect of the heart's possibilities on another plane.

It is often understood in terms of its expression of divinity. And for some, the knowledge and experience of the divine is the only reason for human love to exist—in its representation of the divine on earth. As writer C. S. Lewis contends, "Human loves deserved to be called loves at all just in so far as they resembled the love which is God."

This kind of spiritualized love was first described in ancient Greece and was called *agape*—the opposite of *eros*—meaning "nonerotic." It was really a description of the religious love relationship: the devotion of the worshiper for the worshiped. Agape love was known as a love that liberates, that does not possess, as a source of perfection and spiritual energy.

But spiritual love does not have to take on the value of the divine and the "godly." In his studies on love, Maslow found it unnecessary to distinguish between the spirituality of godly love and the spirituality of human love. He pointed out that the attempt to differentiate the two was usually based on the misunderstanding that pure admiration and "objective" devotional love could be only superhuman qualities, not normal human ones.

Spiritual love might also be characterized as the most refined form of sexual love—a form considered in other eras to be most satisfying. Spiritual love relationships are difficult for us to consider today, but in other eras the experience of this spiritual love between man and woman, contends Richardson, "was so startling and so satisfying that for a thousand years the practice of perpetual virginity was chosen as the way to love more fully."[5]

As celibacy is one way of expressing sexual love in its most universal, most spiritualized state, it is often a testimony to a spiritual commitment. In one sense, spiritual love forces us to surrender all weaknesses and limitations in the personality by creating a condition for bringing out "the best" in us. And as sexuality becomes a restriction in the expression of one's true self, it too must be surrendered to a higher form of expression. It is a vital and necessary part of self-development. To accept one's spiritual needs and desires is as necessary for one's personal growth as the acceptance of one's sexuality. Both are part of developing the ability to love and the capacity for intimacy.

Union: The Goal of Love

> And neither the angels in Heaven above
> Nor the drones down under the sea
> Can ever dissever my soul from the soul
> Of the beautiful Annabel Lee.

———EDGAR ALLEN POE

The goal of all love is said to be growth to the point of full merging of the "souls" or full development of consciousness to experience union—and to live in unity with all aspects of nature, whether with one other human being or all things in the universe.

Until this awareness of union is appreciated, a person may have tried for union only through sexual union. But as one matures, a different view of personal union may start to develop—a union based on spiritual love.

The concept of union or merging with the divine is found in most religions. God is thought to be everywhere and in everything, so it is possible to merge with the divine always, as long as one has first established oneself as a separate expression of divinity. Once the divine self is realized, God is indeed seen everywhere and the individual self, surrender-ing, is "dissolved like a lump of salt in the ocean" but, at the same time, takes on the status of the ocean. And in all spir-itual experiences, once one has recognized divinity, it is in-evitable that one will want to know more of it. This desire is what propels the continuing growth of love; it is the impetus to merge with someone you love or even the whole universe on a much deeper basis than a physical connection. This feel-ing, writes Elizabeth Haich, "has nothing to do with sexual desire, nothing whatsoever to do with the body, for we cer-tainly have no sensual-sexual desire towards the whole wide world, and yet the feeling is there: a purely spiritual feeling, a purely spiritual state."[6]

This growth of love is understandably a real substitute for and even an improvement over sex. And it gives us an in-sight into why some people are willing and able to love and live celibately.

In the following two chapters, celibacy for men and for women is explored in light of particular physical, psychological, and social insights and information specific to each sex. Each chap-ter focuses both on the aftermath of the sexual revolution and the current shift to a more moderate and in some cases, a more celibate, life for both heterosexual and homosexual men and women. There are also personal interviews with men and women who have been celibate for some time and who share their reactions to that experience. With a few exceptions, they were all interviewed in 1979, prior to the emergence of AIDS, and therefore their reasons for choosing celibacy are not fear-based. For the most part, they are individuals who are celi-bate for positive and often spiritual reasons and who are enjoying the results. Although the current interest in being celibate to avoid illness is discussed, along with the specific behavioral changes for gay men in particular, the focus is on the *benefits* of celibacy whether chosen as a preventative mea-sure or as a condition for personal growth.

All of those interviewed had had sexual experience—some

more and some less extensive than average. None seemed to really dislike sex; rather, the emphasis was on enjoying other things more. They considered their celibacy a natural part of their own personal growth, something inevitable, based on a combination of internal and external factors, but definitely something of their own choosing. Most were involved in some kind of program of self-development, although no program had directed them to become celibate. That seemed to be a decision arising out of their own life experiences. In general, they were into healthy living: good food, exercise, no drugs, and so on.

Many felt celibacy offered valuable opportunities for growth in their relationships and within themselves but were not interested in promoting it as a "cause." They considered themselves private explorers, not social innovators. However, those who knew other celibate people felt that this was an important factor in their continuing commitment. They liked the idea of being able to talk about celibacy in a supportive environment with other people who were celibate. None thought that they would necessarily be celibate forever; the overall approach seemed to be to maintain it as long as it provided positive benefits in their lives.

The Celibate Man

MEN, SEX, AND INTIMACY

4 To be intimate, men in our society must deal with overcoming the limitations of lifelong societal lessons on how to be a successful and happy man. There is of course a new kind of man who has surfaced via the women's movement, epitomized best perhaps by talk-show host Phil Donahue and actor Alan Alda: manly and sensitive, strong and emotionally expressive, respectful of women. But most men have found it difficult to integrate the lessons of manliness with those of intimacy, especially in light of male socialization in our society. Under the prevailing mythology, the most pervasive lesson is that masculinity is sexual, and performance and equipment count for almost the whole ballgame. There is little doubt that most men today are intent upon being not just lovers but good lovers. Unfortunately, there's wide disagreement about what that may mean. Many men and even a few women assume that being a good lover means simply being a good "performer."

As a result, most of the qualities associated with masculine sexuality have come to be equated with masculinity in general. A "real" man performs correctly if (1) he has a sexual desire, (2) he has an erection, and (3) he has an orgasm. Feelings of love and tenderness are fine but optional.

When we say a man is soft, we usually mean that he's not altogether there. He can easily be fooled, as in "he's a soft touch" or he's mentally ill as in "he's soft in the head." In general, to be soft is to be a failure if you are a man. Not just sexually but in every way. A real *man*, "The Man of La Macho," is hard, tough as nails. Just as it's good to be hard when you're sexually aroused, it's good to be hard when your emotions, intimate feelings, and desires are on the line. This distortion of male development has presented men in this society with a major dilemma. By concentrating his emotional capabilities on a sexual focus, a man must restrict his full range of expression to those qualities considered right for sexual activity specifically (i.e., hardness, performance) and certainly even limited there.

By restricting masculinity and male image to the sexual arena, self-image becomes overly sexualized. In this way, fears and anxieties stemming from other aspects of male growth settle here. Sex becomes almost the only acceptable measure of male success and, consequently, of alleviating other, non-sexual tensions.

If sexual activity is the modus operandi of being male, then men must be taught to avoid other less "manly" forms of self-expression. And indeed they are—from infancy on. As Ashley Montagu points out in his writings on love and intimacy, girl babies receive more affection through touch than boys. He sees this tactile deprivation reflected later in the typical roughness of the male during lovemaking.

As the sexual becomes the only acceptable channel for male intimacy to express itself, deeper needs for intimacy become repressed or unexpressed. Unable to express himself in the deeper levels of intimate loving, a man may become fearful of these deeper levels and intimacy-related anxieties develop which he feels he must avoid at all costs. *Quite simply, sex can become a way for a man to avoid intimacy and the expression of a more profound part of himself.* And thus sex takes on an additional burden, that of relieving anxiety in men who have been taught that sexual tension means a possible confrontation with their deeper needs.

For many men, therefore, sex is used, quite apart from fulfilling sexual desires, to avoid intimacy, relieve anxiety, cover fears, and express a man's full development as a masculine person. It is little wonder that most men have some uneasiness regarding their sexual abilities. What has been most valued—the male orgasm—may turn out to deserve less value. But as of now, orgasm is *the* predominant goal of male sexuality.

Male Orgasm

If the importance of female orgasm has been under emphasized, to say the very least, the importance of male orgasm has been greatly exaggerated.

——SHERE HITE

According to the Kinsey research, unmarried males between the ages of sixteen and twenty years ejaculate an average of three times a week or about once every two days. Kinsey found daily orgasm to be "well within the capacity of the young male." Married men had the highest number of orgasms per week (about five) but after age thirty, two times a week was the average. For men over seventy, it was found to be about once every two weeks. Other studies have demonstrated that, in general, male sexuality and potency continue even beyond the seventies as long as the brain chemistry and chemical circuits to other parts of the body still respond to sexual arousal.

So it is apparent that if you are a male, having orgasms is not too big a deal. It is likely that you have the capability to have them all your life if you want. Indeed, even the nerds have them. In his film *Manhattan*, the ever neurotic Woody Allen character, responding to a woman's concern that after she finally had her first orgasm her doctor informed her that it was the wrong kind, says, "Mine are always the right kind. Even my worst one was right on the money!"

Yet even though men have them easily enough, orgasms

have somehow become a tremendous sexual goal for men. In our culture, for a man to have an erection and lose it through orgasm is considered to be, by and large, the definition of male sexuality and, consequently, male virility and masculinity. This orgasm focus often continues throughout a man's life, even when it is not socially necessary for procreation or for good sex.

Male Fantasy

It is often assumed that women are the romanticizers and fantasizers, the dreamers and emotional pushovers. However, in her study of romantic love, Dr. Elaine Walster found that men are really more romantic than women. She noted that it is men who fall in love more quickly and women who are more careful and practical when it comes to a romantic commitment. Although women are most involved and consumed at the height of a passionate affair, men tend to be more attached and to cling to a waning romance with greater desperation.

Furthermore, male sexuality has been commonly understood to be oriented to physical need, whereas female sexuality has been thought to be more emotionally based, relying on fantasy for initiating desire. In actuality, men have been found to have far more sexual fantasies and a far greater emotional commitment to sex than women—most likely due to cultural bias favoring sex for men.

And if they can't live out sex in reality, many men lead full and complex sex lives on the level of fantasy. Women tend to think less about sex when they are not involved in a sexual relationship, whereas men tend to continue to think about it. It has been reported that many men really want to escape from the bonds of fantasy living; some even say they have sex simply in order to be free from sexualizing for a time afterward. It isn't sexual activity per se that they want to be free of; it's the tendency to waste time thinking about sex—a kind of never-ending mental loop continually rewound through life-long habits and cultural reinforcement.

Looking more deeply at the ability of men to fantasize about sex, one finds an important understanding about male sexuality that may have been overlooked: the interior ability of men to completely govern their own sexuality—sexuality that has often been viewed as quite automatic and uncontrollable. In fact, it has been found that some men, with proper training, can fantasize physical orgasms (and can achieve multiple orgasms in this way). In his research on spinal-cord–injured individuals, Dr. Theodore Cole found a number of cord-injured men who could achieve each mental state of the progression to orgasm and experience the sensation of its physical counterpart from excitation through ejaculation.

In interviewing one such man—a twenty-seven-year-old video engineer named Richard—the author learned that he was able to transfer his sensual/sexual energy from the lower disabled part of his body to the upper part, particularly his chest area. What was significant was that he was also able to realize an ability to shift this energy anywhere in his body, even entirely to his mind. Here are some of his comments:

> I have ways of rechanneling my genital sexual energy, but I have a lot to learn sexually about myself even after two years of being disabled. I think I am more aware of women on a deeper level since my response is more a psychological release. I maintain a very intense level of feeling, and I have this driving energy which seems to have a lot of power. Instead of diminishing it through genital release like I used to, it seems to get greater. Recently, I had my first orgasm learned in this way. I concentrated my energy on my chest, but I know I could train any part of my body to respond sexually. It feels as though I am expanding to experience the full force of the energy. I watch it happen while I experience it and forget that there is an act or an experience. I seem to go beyond that spectrum.

I'm not bowled over by a physical release, but I do experience a profound warmth and lightness spreading throughout my body.

I feel I have unlimited energy. A lot of my physical energy goes into sports, i.e., wheelchair basketball. I had never really used my body before the accident, and now I really enjoy using it.

I also find that my energy goes into my mental and creative work. I can spend six or seven hours at a time focusing on what I am doing without getting spaced out. I also notice that more and more I can intuitively know things I want to know—I've always had some ability like this, but now I use it much more.

I also think that I have a lot of personal attraction for others. People seem to be drawn to me even when I'm just sitting quietly. I don't think it's because I'm in a wheelchair—more because I feel very stable; my energy feels very self-contained, and I must radiate some of that.

This energy-transfer ability is an indication that men in the Western world have a far greater capacity for experiencing their sexual energy in other than genital ways than they have been taught to imagine. In the East, however, masculinity and virility are understood to be the result of rechanneling sexual energy into higher pursuits. Conservation of this energy and the corresponding physical retention of the seminal fluid are considered imperative in a man's growth toward spiritual fulfillment and enlightenment.

Throughout Western history, a more narrow view of man's physical debilitation resulting from sexual excess is a common theme. In the twelfth century, the Jewish philosopher and physician Moses Maimonides warned: "Effusion of semen represents the strength of the body and its life and the light of the eyes. Whenever it is emitted to excess, the body becomes consumed, its strength terminates, and its life perishes." He goes on to say that excessive sex can cause premature lapses in memory, mental debility, faulty digestion, and defective vision.

Similarly, in the first decades of this century in America, the "alarming" results of male sexual excess were presented by a number of physicians, often in connection with a holistic approach to health, including the need for nutritional programs such as vegetarianism, some form of exercise, and an appeal to renounce liquor and smoking as well as sex.

One such physician, Dr. Arthur Gould, wrote a lengthy treatise on the ill effects of too much sex and despaired: "Modern man cannot be convinced that his perpetual appetite for indulgence is not perfectly natural, even praiseworthy." And only fifty years ago, another writer gloomily detailed: "The too great loss of the seminal fluid soon produces upon men effects very analogous with those of castration, such as weakness, dejection of mind, debility, and pusillanimity, together with all that mental timidity which exaggerates the least dangers and succumbs under the most trivial apprehensions."[1]

In other words, too much sex may make Jack not simply a dull boy but a paranoid schizophrenic. But if a man is celibate, observed Dr. Gould, the "excessive secretions of the vital fluids decrease and are absorbed into the ductless glands," and the energy is maintained—a process which he said restored the experiences of early youth prior to sexual activity.

This line of thought sounds pretty arcane to us now, but the question is whether the recent emphasis on "use it or lose it" is any less naïve. Just because modern researchers have not found any major debilitating effects of sexual activity in the average man does not mean that some effects do not exist in some men. As a matter of fact, very little is known about the physical effects of sexuality in the individual male.

In general, sexual arousal and activity leading to orgasm produce rapid physiological changes. Heart rate doubles, breath rate triples, blood pressure rises considerably. The body must work. Seminal fluid has been found to contain biologically significant nutrients, and a continuous flow of sperm is produced as the blood flows through the testes (where a temperature four degrees cooler than the rest of the body is maintained). During an average ejaculation, one-half billion sperm are released from the body. (After intercourse, it takes a single sperm about thirty minutes to reach the womb.)

It has been found that the amount of seminal fluid is related to the subjective quality of the orgasm. Kinsey's research demonstrated that if a man is low on seminal fluid, the orgasm will not feel as enjoyable. He also found that preadolescent boys have the ability to have multiple orgasms, an ability they tend to lose "at the age when the male climax starts to be accompanied by the ejaculation of semen." So there is a relationship at least between the amount saved and the amount spent in regard to the quality of the sexual experience.

Now it may be true that a lot of sex "can't hurt," but it is also true that many men do feel some weakening effects following ejaculation, often even for a day or two afterward. Each man's individual physiology must be taken into account. The point is that to dismiss a man's postsexual fatigue as a mental rather than physical problem is to neglect all the possible physiological realities of any particular body. It's really no different to declare that all men feel good after sex than to say that all men become weakened and paranoid afterward.

A related consideration of male sexual functioning is the effect of celibacy.

THE REALITIES OF CELIBACY: CAN MEN DO WITHOUT SEX?

Because seminal fluid is produced continuously in a man's body, at times its abundance may cause a physical tension. It is this physical tension which has brought about the misunderstanding that men "need" sex and cannot be celibate.

In reality, in studying the effects of the retention of seminal fluid, Kinsey reported that in comparing celibate men with sexually active men, he did *not* find more nocturnal emissions or any other spontaneous indicators of the male need for physical relief through ejaculation. Kinsey further observed that there is no physiological reason for a man to have real physical discomfort from lack of sexual release: "There is a popular opinion that the testes are the sources of the semen which the male ejaculates. The testes are supposed to become swollen with accumulated secretions between the times of sexual activity, and periodic ejaculation is supposed to be necessary in order to relieve these pressures....Most of these opinions are, however, quite unfounded."[2]

Kinsey goes on to say that if there is discomfort as the result of unrelieved erotic arousal, it is located in the surrounding musculature and not in the testes and/or sexual organs themselves. And obviously, if sexual arousal does not occur regularly, there can be no reason for any physical difficulties.

What Kinsey did find was that men in situations requiring celibacy are much more comfortable than expected. For one thing, without external sexual stimuli, male sexual desire tends to diminish. Kinsey's research of sex in prison life in the 1940s led to his observation that when men are in non-erotic situations or environments (for example, short-term prison), they adjust to celibacy even for a year at a time. "Most of them live comfortably enough apparently because there is little erotic arousal which needs to be relieved by orgasm."

For another thing, as time goes on, the less sex men engage in, the less they desire it. The longer a man is celibate, the easier it becomes for him to be celibate. In his research on male sexuality, Dr. Bernard Zilbergeld found that men who are celibate are not plagued by "consuming sexual appetites." Shere Hite reached similar conclusions—that men don't really need sex as often as they think they do.

In addition, men may think they need sex because even if they were physically comfortable, their fantasies would overwhelm them. In this regard, some men interviewed for a *New*

York Times article on celibacy expressed interest in celibacy but were afraid to try it for fear of having to live with *more* sexual fantasies.

As more research on male sexuality and celibacy is carried out, more detailed documentation of the effects of both on a man's health and activities will enable us to have a more complete picture.

The Sexuality of the Older Man

As a man gets older, the orgasm mode of sexual functioning is still understood to be the "correct" expression of a man's vitality and ability to love. Even though older men have less physical desire to have an orgasm, the psychological dependence that has been created throughout a lifetime may never diminish. Thus a great fear of adult males in our society is of the "male menopause"—a time when procreative genital function has changed to a more diffuse sexuality—and many men despair that they will become less manly, less sexual, and therefore, less alive.

Joseph Wade, in his studies of sex and celibacy in church life, distinguished between a physical desire for sexual expression which he, like Kinsey, observed to diminish after age thirty and a psychological "need" for sex based on social training, which may never diminish.

Thus, as men get older, many find that their sexual needs continue, although the need is generally psychological rather than somatic.

For an older man, celibacy may seem to be more a reluctant resignation than a real choice. It is definitely considered a choice for a younger man who is thought to be functioning at full sexual steam and therefore has something to be celibate about. But an older man may see celibacy as a final defeat in his battle to uphold waning virility. This is a very unfortunate distortion. For once masculinity and virility are seen for what they really are, sexuality may become a *restriction* of their development.

The value of age—with its accompanying realization of

who one is and what one wants, of wisdom, of the release from the social straits of "what others think of me," of the profound vision of seeing what one's real commitments in life are: these are the glory of the older man. Certainly men can feel sexy and have orgasms even in their eighties, but to hold on to that limited view of self-worth when one has finally reached a pinnacle of fullness in life—this can really diminish a man's strength and status in the world.

Few things are as embarrassing as one age trying to be another. Just as we feel uncomfortable around somber, adult-like children "wise beyond their years," we naturally feel uncomfortable around men or women trying to be adolescents—not only for the futility of their efforts, but also for the waste of their precious adulthood in favor of a less developed status.

A virile man is one who is what he is—fully established in his own being—not one who tries to be what he was at a younger age thereby denying his present self.

A broader vision of manliness that presents men with a more complete picture of the nature of virility, of strength, of masculine prowess is needed. In this regard, it is useful to look at some other views of male sexuality and celibacy.

The Macho Celibate: The Masculine Virtue of Sexual Abstinence

In our culture, male celibacy has been generally associated with strict religious vocation or with extenuating social situations such as wartime or the death of a spouse. Not until recently has any thought been given to *choosing not* to express one's maleness through sexuality. But in most other times and cultures, the expression of male sexuality has not been the exclusive basis for proving oneself to be a man: in other words, what has been considered truly masculine, strong, and virile has not been ordinarily confined to sexual activity.

Although there has been a widespread tendency for cultures to equate male sexuality with power, in most societies such power has been equated not with the participation in sexual activity but with the *withholding* of sexuality. "Celibate prowess," not sexual prowess, has been most often regarded as the real proving ground for the challenge of masculine strength.

Such an attitude may emerge in a given society following prior excessive sexual activity. As Bertrand Russell wrote in *Marriage and Morals,* "Men who are not restrained by a fairly rigid ethic are apt to indulge to excess: This produces in the end a feeling of weariness... which leads naturally to ascetic convictions." Obviously, the pendulum has swung back many times before: There have been many "lusty" societies in the history of the world for which celibacy must have provided a welcome relief. For example, in ancient Rome, despite its dissolute reputation, the effort of continence was greatly admired and thought to represent a superior nature and a character verging on the divine.

Courtly Love: The Male Celibate Tradition

Perhaps the most notable period of male secular celibacy occurred during the Middle Ages when the tradition of courtly love was at its height and when masculine sexuality was successfully transformed into devotional service and spiritual love. It was the duty of the knight to devote himself unselfishly to the noble lady. The knight would thus offer his full strength to his lady for whom he fought in battle and for whom he contained his sexuality. This ritual of the Middle Ages was called *māze*—the power of devotional love created by the withholding of sexual activity.

In his description of the courtly love tradition, which later came to be called the tradition of romantic love, Dr. Hugo Beigel writes: "In spite of the surface appearance of its aesthetic formulation, it sprang from vital needs, from a deeply-felt desire for the ennoblement of human relations.... It made māze (or moderation) a masculine virtue."[3]

But the actual arrangements between the knights and their

ladies occurred only *outside* marriage: "Being the spiritualization and the sublimation of carnal desire, such love was
deemed to be impossible between husband and wife." This
was due to the Christian idea that sex was wholly incompat-
ible with spirituality; in this light a sexual marriage had no
place for spiritual growth. These spiritually elevating relations
could, therefore, only be established between the knight and
the lady. This arrangement for a spiritual relationship was
called *minne* and was based on absolute chastity. Within the
tradition, the woman was idealized and elevated. Respect for
her high position induced devotion, tenderness, and restraint
in the male worshiper. For the woman, loyalty to her husband was separate from her loyalty to her gallant. Of course,
being married, she herself was not able to be celibate; she was
merely an object of love through which the knight could
achieve his own uplift. In such a state, the knight's love was
said to flower and, indeed, bring about spiritual experiences
and increasingly higher planes of devotional feeling.

Safely kept from sexual expression, so-called "love tests"
were undertaken by the lovers. The test of *drutz* was considered the "Black Belt" of courtly love—the highest state of the
art. The knight or gallant was allowed into the lady's bed
chamber, permitted to undress her completely, to put her to
bed, and even to kiss her and sleep with her in a nonsexual
embrace.

This spiritualized love actually opened the way for the later
tradition of romantic love, which still later became sexualized.
But advocates of the courtly love or romantic tradition devoid
of sexual activity consider it one of the high points in the history of love of men for women.

THE TREND TO CELIBACY: WHY MEN DO WITHOUT SEX

In the early 1950s, in his research on celibacy, Albert C. Kinsey
found that in men under the age of thirty, abstinence was common for a few days or a week at a time, but only 11 percent

reported being abstinent for longer than two weeks at a time and only 3 percent were abstinent for ten weeks or longer. Kinsey further observes, however, that most men he interviewed would have been ashamed to report any lack of sexual activity because the social pressure to be sexually active was too great. So he was not convinced of the accuracy of those figures.

In their book *The Virile Man*, Sheldon Fellman and Paul Neimark see celibacy as a very positive alternative for some men. Dr. Fellman, a urologist, has found about one in every thirty or forty men to be "unconcerned with sex"; often he is "a man who wants to devote all his energies to his work."

Isaac Newton, Immanuel Kant, William Pitt, Martin Luther, Beethoven, Sigmund Freud, Anthelme Brillat-Savarin, George Bernard Shaw, Henry David Thoreau, and Alfred Hitchcock are some well-known men who practiced celibacy for all or part of their lives. There have no doubt been many successful secular celibates who did not necessarily give up social life or even marriage in order to remain nonsexual. In all likelihood, male celibacy has become more acceptable as more men find it useful in their lives. Its usefulness ranges from a cure for impotence to a commitment of all sexual energy for spiritual life.

Celibacy has been a recognized cure for impotence for centuries. In his writings on male sexuality, Maimonides prescribed celibacy as the necessary antidote to impotence resulting from a variety of causes including sexual fatigue. And today, a large number of doctors and therapists are recommending celibacy for men to help alleviate the stress associated with sex and the pressure to perform in specified ways. Celibacy is said to "center" the impotent man by allowing him to stay within himself, to rest, to regroup his resources, and to rechannel his blocked energy.

There may be a tendency to want to relate impotence with the new celibacy, but they are totally different—in fact, celibacy is very much the opposite of impotence. An impotent man generally wants to have sex but cannot perform, whereas a celibate man generally can perform but does not want to have sex. Indeed, celibacy can be considered "the source of the very highest potency." Haich describes the enlightened celibates whose energies have been directed to other than sexual goals. The body, she says, at these higher energy levels, "lives with much greater intensity and has much greater potency than the body of a man who is still in the grip of sexuality and expends life-giving energy." Furthermore, she emphasizes that "these enlightened men did not become impotent, no matter how often ignorant people may claim the contrary."

Male Celibacy and Relationships

Eugene Bianchi, a Jesuit who was celibate for twenty years prior to marriage, studied celibacy within the church and observed a distinction between physical celibacy and what he calls psychic celibacy. He says that the psychic celibate keeps women at arm's length, not only physically but mentally and emotionally as well. Women are seen primarily as embodiments of the "temptress"; in order to maintain psychic celibacy, women are excluded on *all* levels of relating.

It's true that quite a few men see women as exclusively sexual—and are thus unable to separate their emotional relationships with women from the sexual components. And if they become celibate, they think that they must keep entirely separate from women. One scientist interviewed by the *New York Times* reported that after a year of being celibate, what he missed most was "not sex but the closeness you feel in a primary relationship." It is unfortunate that his understanding of closeness and sexuality were so intricately bound that he did not feel he had the opportunity to experience a close relationship while celibate.

The truth of the matter is that, for many men, celibacy can be a great help for allowing growth in relationships without the set patterns imposed by sexual habits and expectations.

And, interestingly, celibate men who are open to relating to women find that women are very attracted to them. There seems to be a kind of personal strength and charisma that celibate men manifest. A man who has freely chosen to be celibate and is comfortable with it offers other people the chance to see themselves reflected in his eyes and heart in other than sexual ways. It's a great gift to "see" and "be seen" without the imposition of the dominating sexual viewpoint.

Celibacy can help a man explore new modes of personal communication and intimate relating with others. It can also enable a man to pursue a variety of goals such as deepening his commitment to achievement in work or spending more time with his children or other perhaps more spiritual goals. Celibacy can provide a way for a man to open his heart to his lovers, friends, and family; to break boundaries in his own emotional life; to get more deeply involved with his own nonsexual priorities. It can help a man envision his life more clearly, take control of his activities, learn to choose what he wants and who he wants it with. It can help him take charge of his mind and his body, and it can enable him to come to grips with his masculinity by allowing him to separate his virility from his sexuality.

In all, celibacy can both strengthen a man and soften him; it can allow him to experience the unboundedness of his settled being, to experience the expansion of his heart and mind into other areas of relating and accomplishing. He can deepen his life without losing his focus on personal growth at the expense of a habit he no longer wants to be bound by. Celibacy can free him to look at his own sexual life, to put in perspective what place he wants sex to have in his daily experience and to find what other possibilities are available to him.

FIVE CELIBATE MEN
INTERVIEWED IN 1979

Carl: Age Twenty-eight, Auto Salesman

"I have been celibate for two years, since my divorce. I was married for three and a half years and when the marriage was over, I went through a heavy 'proving' time, making sure I was still desirable and sexy to women. I actually looked up my old high school flames and had several affairs. I have always been a real 'mover' sexually—always looking for the next sexual experience before I was even finished with the current one.

"I do remember just when I decided to be celibate. I was driving late one night, and I stopped at a traffic light. My window was rolled down, and this girl at the corner came up and asked me if I wanted a date. It turned me on, and we ended up in bed and I got VD. I felt really unpleasant—had some nasty moments at the doctor's office—'Oh, you're the one with the gonorrhea,' etc. I decided that it was really ridiculous to be so dominated by sex that I really ended up feeling miserable. Somehow this experience was a sign that I'd better take a little responsibility for myself and what I was doing. So I decided intellectually to be celibate.

"I say intellectually because I am still very sexual. But, lo and behold, I found that I could contain my sexual impulses pretty easily and be free of that constant push to get into bed with someone. I found that the desire would awaken, but if I didn't act on it, it wouldn't be as strong. Every time I was horny and didn't 'do it,' either find a woman to sleep with or masturbate, I wouldn't be as horny the next time the desire came up. I did stop masturbating almost entirely and feel good about that.

"When I am happy, it's very easy to be celibate. When I'm unhappy, it's more difficult, and I start to get sexually turned on. I know that I have pretty much used sex as a way to relieve frustration in other areas of my life, even when I was married. I think that being celibate has given me a great deal more stability in my life and allowed me to have much better relationships with women. You'd be surprised how many women are drawn to a celibate man. It gives them a chance to be themselves without sex and still be loved.

"I don't know how much longer I'll be celibate. I basically take it on a day-to-day basis. I don't want to feel like I'm holding back some part of me, but I do think by consciously avoiding sex, I've opened up a whole new field for my personality to express itself. And I do feel a lot better about myself.

"Am I uncomfortable physically, not being sexually active? No, not at all. If I don't put myself in a tempting situation, I don't get turned on and I avoid the frustration. The whole feeling is very liberating for a man."

Brent, Age Twenty-four, Graduate Student

"I've never been in love the way I fantasize love. I spent about six years trying to live out my fantasies, and it didn't really work. I've thought about sex since I was very young. I think I've been more sexually consumed in fantasy than most men.

"The big thing in college of course has been 'progressive' sex—how far you can go and how soon—i.e., 'scoring.' Consequently, most of my sexual experience has been 'one-nighters.' Until I was twenty, I was part of the 'if-it-feels-good, do-it' school. I probably slept with about forty different women. Usually, I separated my women 'friends' from my sexual companions. Like I'd say, 'She means more to me as a friend.' I guess I must have thought it was more of a compliment to a girl not to have sex with her.

"Then I met a woman with whom I had a long-term affair—a year and a half—based pretty much on sex. I wasn't in love with her, but I was comfortable with her. There wasn't a lot of guilt. It was a real time of sexual exploration but also a realization that I wanted more than sex from a relationship. We were very different: sex is what kept us together, but, basically, I was bored. Eventually, sex wasn't enough. After we broke up, I almost started being promiscuous again, but somehow it didn't have the same pull as before. It seems that I had to choose between promiscuity and celibacy. So I've been celibate for about a year.

"There's a part of me that would hop into anyone's bed, and there's a stronger part of me that wants to find someone who turns me on more than sexually. It's easy to turn me on sexually. I know, however, that I want to take my time and really find what I want and get to know someone. It's hard to put out energy and not have it come back.

"I've been getting closer to my male friends as the result of this period of celibacy. It seems that because I'm not being sexual, I'm not as threatened getting close to men. At the same time, I think I'm getting closer to women. I live with a woman who has a child and even though it's nonsexual, I really enjoy the warmth of a kind of family life with her.

"I used to get sex confused with other things. I was really tied into how others see me. My worth was verified by someone wanting to have sex with me, so not having sex made me feel deprived. Now, sex for me has got to be connected with another person, with emotions; it can't just be sex for sex's sake. My standards for what I want have gotten higher, I think. I'm more concerned with the quality of how I feel about the person.

"Since I've been celibate, sex is less on my mind than it used to be. This surprised me because I thought I'd think more about it. I actually have fewer sexual fantasies than before. It was too frustrating and as I started having other activities in other areas, the fantasies went away. I think I became more involved in other parts of my life. Masturbation too has decreased from once a day to less than once a week. It seems that it's easier for me to forego sex now than when I first stopped having it.

"I know I haven't given up sex. I'm just looking for the right person to share it with. I'm interested in getting married and having a family, and I guess that, strange as it may seem, this time of celibacy is preparing me for that kind of commitment. Otherwise, I'd still be running around with as many women as I could find to get it on with. And I'd still be feeling worthless and frustrated. This way, I feel like even though I'd rather be involved with someone than not, it's in my own best interest to be celibate until I find what I am looking for, and not waste my time, energy, and thoughts on unrewarding people and experiences."

John: Age Twenty-seven, Architect

"I've been celibate for about a year and have been openly gay for over seven years. Before that I had some not-too-successful experiences with women. I lived with one man for two and one-half years and have definitely had my share of sexual experiences with other men.

"When I decided to be celibate, it was an impulsive kind of thing—as if to say 'Stop all this nonsense.' I had begun to feel really trapped by what I consider pretty typical gay male behavior. Maybe it's also typical of other people, I don't know. Basically, it seemed that the possibilities of relating to another man who is also gay begin with sex and end when sex ends. I know this isn't just true for me. Of course, I do know some gay couples for whom sex has become just one part of the relationship, and I even know a completely celibate gay couple, but in my experience, most gays are largely dominated by sexual relating at the expense of other kinds.

"Once you've experienced the exhilaration and freedom of expressing love for your own sex, you realize how great a distance is yet to go. Many gays, once they've come out, tend to stop relating beyond sex. In a way, it was a lot more interesting to meet other men before it was so acceptable to be gay. Mainly because there was no guarantee that sex was going to be part of the experience, and you would spend a lot of time getting to know each other before the 'big revelation.' I think gay life is so sexual because that's the part of the personality which is identified. It seems really unfair to me. I like sex, don't get me wrong, but I really get off on the emotional involvement with men.

"I read an interview with Quentin Crisp—the man on whom the TV play *The Naked Civil Servant* was based. I saved it and would like to have some of it quoted because I agree with what he says, and I think he says it very well, if a little intensely.

> As soon as you know a person, sex is over. All married couples find this. You may seek sex elsewhere,

but your relationship is no longer supported by its sexuality.... With homosexuals, it's more extreme. They try to find situations in which the person with whom they are having some kind of sexual relationship cannot have time to utter a word for fear they would reveal something about themselves and become a person.

If you are happy, you don't pursue sex in this frantic way. Whether you are sexually happy is not the point. If you're happy, if you have a nice life, if you do a job that other people tell you you do well, then you live contentedly. Sex is an illness, a fever. And this perpetual search for pleasure is always undertaken by people who have no happiness.[4]

"Since I've been celibate, some good things have been growing in me. For one thing, I've stopped relating to people in a predominantly sexual way—I've stopped relating to men as sexual objects and women as sexual threats. I've also more or less forced others to see *me* in other ways, too. Which has been very important to me.

"I like relating to women as a celibate man. It takes a lot of the tension away because it takes the sexual 'challenge' of homosexuality away. Women I know were often out to be the one who reforms me. Now it's a more natural kind of relating. They see me now not as a disappointment but as a man with a lot to offer them that other men don't give them. And with straight men too I'm more comfortable. If they're threatened by me, I know it's their trip because I know I'm not doing any challenging.

"So I feel much more open in all my relationships. I feel like I've grown a lot emotionally, become stronger, more independent. My work has really progressed, and I've had much more opportunity to get into it in a profound way. I don't know if that has to do with being celibate, but I have noticed that my attention is much more solid and focused, and I feel more calm inside. I don't know how long I'll remain celibate, but it's certainly been good for me. Some friends were very skeptical about my motivations at first—they thought it was sort of phony, but they've definitely changed their opinion since they've seen me change and now they too seem interested in being less involved in sex and more involved in living a more balanced life."

Patrick: Age Sixty-one, Research Director

"I've been celibate for two and a half years, since my divorce. I was married for twenty years, and we have four children. I would say that the main desires I have in my life are the pursuit of my work and taking care of my family. My time is very precious to me—to pursue a woman to have an affair or to have a future commitment—these are not part of my interests right now. I have no desire to be remarried.

"Several years before the divorce, my time became very limited. My work had become more and more absorbing and also enjoyable. We had an excellent sex life together, but my wife wanted more time together—certainly a natural desire for her but a difficult one for me. I seemed to want less of a sexual relationship than she did—it didn't seem to be spontaneous in light of our limited time together. The real reasons for our divorce were not problems of sex but problems of attention—how much I could give to my wife, how much to our children, how much to my work and all the people involved there. This situation hasn't changed much since the divorce.

"I consider my sex life to be 'normal.' I've had sexual experiences for forty years. I think I had average sexual desires, although not much expression in fantasy. My fantasies now aren't generally sexual either. I feel that at this point, the intensity of needs and physiological functioning are over and, truthfully, I'm glad about it. I don't see that being sexual all your life is either necessary or desirable.

"I grew up in a strict Lutheran-Catholic environment. Perhaps I would have been more familiar with and, therefore, more sexual with women if I had had a less religious upbringing, but I don't think so. For one thing, I was a training athlete throughout my youth, and I think I expended my energies toward a commitment to sports and competition. My first sexual encounter was with my first wife when I was twenty-one. I went into the service at age twenty-four and was celibate for three years during the war, but I didn't mind. My attention was in a different place than on sexuality at the time. But I guess celibacy was never as difficult for me as it may be for other men. I really don't know.

"I do enjoy the company of women a great deal. I am attracted to them and they to me. But since I'm not really wanting to pursue a sex-based relationship, I try not to make myself available. I don't seek sex, but I enjoy playing sports with women and working with them in a comfortable, friendly way. When I have some extra time, I play tennis and golf and usually jog about five miles a day if possible. These activities are made more enjoyable by the company of women.

"My basic theory about sex is that the intensity of desire changes as the attention changes and vice versa. At first, male attention is almost entirely on sex. It seems to be a major way men prove themselves. But as you get older, you've experienced so much sex in the past, and you know what it is. Your attention then may shift to other things. I'm at least a semimature creature and don't seem to want to run around looking for sex. I live with a certain amount of ease and peace. For me, sex was deeply connected with family life and children. At this time, sex is not very interesting to me, and I would be forcing it if I tried to make it more important than it is. So celibacy seems very natural. There is really no other choice. And I'm happy with it."

Don: Age Thirty-two, Store Manager

I decided to be celibate just to see what my relations with women would be like. At the time, they weren't very satisfactory. I kept sleeping with women in hopes of falling in love with them. I was forever looking for the 'ideal' woman who would share all my hopes and dreams and look at things the same way as I did. I guess I was very afraid of being open with women. I didn't want them to be different from me because I was too insecure to accept women as different. If I slept with a woman who didn't share the same values, I'd almost have to sit and stare at the wall for two days in order to recover. But since I was pretty obsessed with sex, I slept with anyone I could, not usually going further than sex in the relationship.

"I've been celibate for about eight months. I just decided it was a good way to break a bad pattern of behavior. At first, I noticed a kind of irritability from not having sex regularly, but then I noticed a kind of heightened perception in understanding people. I began to 'see' women as people, maybe for the first time. A funny thing was that women became inordinately attracted to me, perhaps because I gave them a certain kind of attention that was really more powerful than sexual attention.

"I find I don't need to prove myself through sex. Now, sex is not the number one desire nor my main interest with women. I feel more even with them. I still desire a deep mutuality with a woman, and I feel that this goal is more possible now."

The Celibate Woman

A SHORT SEXUAL HISTORY

5 Throughout most of world history, in ancient Persia, in China (even until this century), in Greece—in most of the major civilizations—women have remained uneducated. Bertrand Russell notes:

> In most civilized communities, women have been denied almost all experience of the world and of affairs. They have been kept artificially stupid and, therefore, uninteresting. From Plato's dialogues one derives an impression that he and his friends regarded men as the only proper objects of serious love. This is not to be wondered at when one considers that all the matters in which they were interested were completely closed to respectable Athenian women.[1]

This lack of education is reflected in the lack of sexual knowledge accorded women. Not only were women kept "noneducated," they were also kept "nonsexual." Every so often in history this was not the case but in general, women's sexuality was viewed only in terms of their ability to elicit male sexual response.

109

Women have been credited historically with every vice and with every virtue. Woman has moved from the sexual status of low-down temptress to unearthly saint and back again. Many religions have imbued women with all sorts of sexual powers and then taken them away. A striking example of this dichotomy occurs in Christianity, where one woman (Eve) is the cause of original sin and the fall from grace, and another woman (Mary) is the inspiration for the purity of all devouts—including the celibates of the priesthood.

Historically, women were dependent socially and economically but not sexually upon men. They were not sexually dependent because they were not considered "sexual." Some researchers have speculated that this was because female sexual response was unnecessary for reproduction. Only male orgasm was required, and therefore women's only real sexual function was to serve as what Masters and Johnson have indelicately called "seminal receptacles."

As female sexuality was never even considered apart from marital obligations and childbearing functions, women were not attentive to their own sexual desires—nor was male attention put upon their needs. As a result, women either learned not to be sexual or never learned to *be* sexual.

It is interesting that although modern research in sexuality has revealed women's great sexual capacity (an orgasmic capacity demonstrated to be greater than men's), there is no evidence that women in the past experienced what we call sexual frustration. Not knowing their own sexual natures and not called upon to have sexual lives, they were apparently not disappointed. Author Barbara Seaman maintains that those Victorian women who were "totally unaroused" sexually were nonetheless often in love with their husbands for a lifetime and "were not consciously frustrated."

As women obtained their long-overdue education, they became more knowledgeable about all aspects of life, including their own sexuality. But when women's sexuality was finally acknowledged in America and England a century ago, a great attempt was made to continue to keep women nonsexual.

Thus the Victorian era became synonymous with sexual repression. It was a time in which sexual innocence gave way to sexual knowledge, but in the process both the innocence and the knowledge became falsified.

In an effort to deny what was considered the shocking reality of female sexuality, Victorian society put forth some amazing distortions. Men were said to have "bestial" sexual needs and women had to be protected from them. In fact, Victorian women held a widespread belief that they were morally superior to men *because* they experienced less pleasure in sex. Women were supposed to be completely blind to their own feelings, negating any indication of possible compliance on their part. This extreme denial was so severe that "good" women could not even accept their own organic structures lest the truth be known. It is reported that many women died rather than undergo much-needed gynecological examinations and admit to their own sexual organs. And even as recently as sixty years ago, it was illegal in England to state in print that a wife can and should derive pleasure from sexual activities.

Under these conditions, it is not surprising that sex took on a huge, unnatural significance—far more powerful in such a repressive era than in times when sex is quietly accepted for its own specific role in the culture.

To counteract this absurd distortion came Freud and his theory of sexuality, which represented neurotic and normal behaviors as based on degrees of repression and sublimation of sexuality. Freud's remarkable insights brought about a much-needed opening of awareness and acceptance of human sexuality, but at the same time created other distortions. The unfortunate result of Freud's view of his own age led more recent societies to overvalue sex and its role in human development.

One particular aspect of Freud's theory that was embraced until two decades ago was the biological model of female sexuality which erroneously defined women's capabilities based on incomplete physiological knowledge of how women generally achieve orgasm. This misinformation was later corrected through the work of Dr. Mary Jane Sherfey, Masters and Johnson, and others. But as the result of this prolonged misunderstanding, women who were sexually normal were taught that they were not. This was not as demeaning to women in the days when they were appreciated for their nonsexual functions during the times when marriage and motherhood were glorified. But as that emphasis shifted, and sexual and romantic love became the standard for a woman's social success, the seeming inability to behave as a sexually "normal" woman was a great psychological blow to many women, especially at a time when they were supposed to feel sexually liberated.

This led to a particularly narrow view of women's psychology, perhaps best summarized in the statement by Percival Symonds that "women seek love experiences for the restoration of wounded self-esteem." When the only acceptable role for women to play is a sexual-romantic one and when a woman's worth is based on sexual attractiveness, it is no wonder that women who thought that there was something wrong with them sexually experienced a great deal of social insecurity.

And this transition from being nonsexual to being "abnormal" was no doubt a key factor in the decision of many women finally to determine their own sexuality for themselves and evaluate their sexual needs in terms that men never used—related to independence and self-worth. This in turn led some women to see their sexuality in a somewhat biased fashion—as a key to personality and as a means for personal liberation. During the 1960s, this most likely served as a spur to the women's movement, which attempted to sort out the confused female experience of the sexual revolution.

At the same time, as women's sexual identity shifted from childbearer to sex "object" in response to the societal shift from the family emphasis to the focus on individual love relationships, women found themselves in a very difficult social position. What was meant to be progressive and liberating—the freedom implied by the sexual revolution—may have forced a further restriction on their social lives. This is partly because the role of a sex object or even a sex "subject" is far more limited than even the role of a wife and mother in the opportunity for growth. The mystery of the orgasm had been solved, but the real nature of being a woman remained even more hidden. As Diana Trilling observed:

> I know any number of borderline psychotics who are having perfectly fine sexual lives, in the sense that they have orgasms, lots of them, if that's what you define it by....
>
> I think women are being liberated to be a mess. They have the right to be as much of a mess as men, they really do. But I do think we'd all be a lot better off if we didn't think that to be liberated to be a mess is somehow a fulfillment of our femininity.[2]

WOMEN'S REACTION TO THE SEXUAL REVOLUTION

Most women found the effect of the sexual revolution a mixed blessing. There were, of course, various responses by women to what was seen alternatively as a more liberalized freeing of sexuality to a more restrictive mechanizing of sex-as-orgasm. There were some women who embraced the social freedom of unattached sexuality by mimicking some men who wanted to, if not "have it all" at least "do it all." Reflecting on this indiscriminate behavior, Barbara Seaman wrote: "It has long been argued that it takes three generations to make a natural gentleman. Perhaps by the same token, it will take three generations to make a naturally-liberated woman. Some of the girls who discover sexual freedom are a bit like *nouveau riche* males, at first, expending their wealth universally and with very questionable taste."[3]

Other women applauded some of the results—particularly

the informational benefits—but continued to feel uncomfortable. A precarious balance seemed to emerge: (1) A woman must be careful not to threaten men by being too open about wanting sex and must continue to allow herself to be "seduced" into something she presumably wants anyway, and (2) a woman must be ready and available and willing to have sex in order not to be considered hung-up, antisocial, or repressed. Repression was the worst sin of all. A startling example of the consequences of this concern was reported by newscaster David Brinkley on the NBC Evening News in 1979: One in five American male doctors questioned stated that they believe it is helpful for their female patients if they have erotic contact with them. And a careful nationwide study in 1984 conducted by Nanette Gartrell and Judith Herman, M.D., assistant professors of psychiatry at Harvard Medical School, indicated that, of those willing to admit it, over 7 percent of male psychiatrists and over 3 percent of female psychiatrists have had sexual contact with one or more of their patients.[4]

All in all, the major emphasis to emerge from the sexual revolution was the female orgasm and the achievement thereof; in many ways this further narrowed the already restrictive focus of lovemaking. It became a prime concern not only for women but for men.

As a result, there was some regret for the loss of the less goal-oriented days. As one woman wrote in response to Shere Hite's questionnaire, "The rare times when sex was a tool for healing, or emotional relating, when extra warmth and intimacy were needed, orgasm was unnecessary. Also, before I learned how to have an orgasm, sex was a service of intimacy to my partner."

Anthropologist Margaret Mead observed that female orgasm is not a problem in most primitive cultures, where men are trained to bring women to orgasm as part of their social responsibilities. But in our culture until very recently, while male orgasms were thought of as inevitable, female orgasms were depicted as rare, mysterious, and difficult to achieve, requiring hard work and concentration. In the seventies, a woman learned to "take responsibility" for her orgasms, resulting in a strangely unevolved, goal-oriented attitude. This attitude could be readily traced to the deprivation many women experienced in unsatisfactory sexual relationships. Yet it also served to constrict women's sexuality to the same limited framework which has been the restrictive focus in male sexuality, perhaps prohibiting deeper and fuller experiences from occurring.

It became apparent that women were not as interested in sex as they thought they ought to be. What women seem to be most interested in—fulfillment in relationships and personal growth—was not particularly advanced by the revolution in sexual attitudes. Women found that "good sex and plenty of it" did not bring fulfillment. It simply created a new set of concerns that only replaced but did not to do away with, the problems they faced before the revolution. Said one woman, "If I go for long without sex, my desires drop ridiculously, which worries me. I start to wonder if something is 'wrong' with me, which makes me feel obligated to have sex."[5]

Just as it was a near–social impossibility for a woman to say yes when all society told her to say no, now the very opposite situation confronted her. This confusion was heightened by the accompanying confusion of social roles. Most women did not want to lose men's love and felt that sex was the only way to ensure it. (This situation was further compounded by the demand not only to have sex freely but also to have an orgasm every time.)

Learning to say no was not that easy for most women, but in the process of making that choice, a woman could begin to overcome not only social but personal limitations. As psychoanalyst June Singer wrote:

> In the process of asserting herself and saying *no* for the first time, a woman may learn a great deal. If she is sufficiently committed to the task of increasing her level of consciousness, she may discover that not all

of the opposition is outside, not all is coming from men, not all is coming from the world. Much of it is internal. Woman is bound, at least to some degree, because she allows herself to be bound, and often in the name of love. It is a stage that many creative women have to go through.[6]

And, according to the observations of Masters and Johnson, "A woman cannot be sexually emancipated without first becoming personally emancipated."

Fortunately, most women began to see the limiting effects of orgasm-oriented love and started revealing what they really want.

What Women Really Want

Women want to love and be loved and are apparently more open about that desire than are men. Despite their ability to be more sexual than men, at least in their capacity for multiple orgasms, women in general continue to prefer the emotional to the sexual aspects of their relationships.* Consequently, given a choice between good sex and good emotional contact, women far prefer the latter—the sharing, intimacy, touching, and tenderness.

Touch is very important to most humans, and few people in our society get enough of it. Yet touching is most often used to prepare for sexual activity and not enjoyed simply for its own pleasure. Most women want to touch and be touched, independent of sex.

Therefore, for many women, the emotional satisfactions of

---

*This preference is borne out in Masters and Johnson's research, where it was found that although female orgasm through masturbation is usually more intense and occurs with much greater frequency than orgasm through intercourse, most women prefer the closeness of intercourse because the emotional component of sexuality is far more important to them than orgasm.

intimacy with or without sex are the essence of making love. Physical closeness without physical sex is something that women tend to enjoy and quite a few actually prefer to the experience of orgasm because it incorporates so many of the subtleties of love and romance.

"Women like sex," wrote Shere Hite, "more for the feelings involved than for the purely physical sensations of intercourse per se." Her survey showed that sex is considered important to women because of the intimacy and closeness it allows with another human being—as a way of showing deepest love. This is also why women specifically say they like sexual intercourse, because of the closeness (not necessarily the sexuality) of the physical expression of love. Sex is also considered important because women see it as a way to establish their feelings of security and desirability and as an affirmation of self-worth. Sex is also a time of giving pleasure to a partner—a time of trust and surrender in love.

Most women have been found to respond to sexual activity based on what they have been taught about sex. For women as well as for men, sex is a learned response, even if new learning replaces old lessons. If a woman is taught that sex occurs as foreplay, sexual intercourse, and male ejaculation, this is what she will hold sex to be and will feel "wrong" with another sequence or set of activities. If a woman is taught to view sexual intercourse or the reproductive model of sexuality as exploitive and the female orgasm as the only justifiable reason to engage in sexual activity, this is what sex will be for her and anything else will seem false or limited.

There is little doubt that their nonsexual history still very much affects the thinking of many women. One indicator of this is the difference between men's and women's fantasy lives. Whereas men tend to fantasize more when they are not involved in a relationship, women have been found to think about and fantasize much less about sex when they are not involved. And whereas men will fantasize in order to become aroused, women fantasize in order to become "unaroused"— to achieve orgasm. Strictly physical fantasies focused on the ongoing sexual experience itself are most common. It is also interesting that very few women have any basis for connecting their sexual feelings with other aspects of their lives in fantasy. Nor have they been found to fantasize using more universal or spiritual images.

Perhaps because of their short history of overt sexuality, women seem to be more flexible about sexual desire than do men. For the most part, women have learned to accommodate their sexuality to the situation. This works two ways: On the one side, women don't have to be convinced to have sex. As one woman said, "The reason why so-called seduction practices work is that [a woman] is simply an erotic being in her own right, and with the proper attention and stimulation, she'll be at a point where she'd rather have sex than anything."[7]

On the other side, most women do not report a regular sexual appetite. Shere Hite found that "the appetite for sex with another person became really intense only in relation to desire for a specific person." Many of her respondents reported that when sex wasn't available (when they were not involved in a specific relationship), they tended not to want sex. Her conclusion: "The less you have it, the less you want it."

Orgasm of the Heart

Closer to the experience women describe as most desirable is a more intimate kind of "orgasm" or melting of feeling, which sometimes occurs during sex and sometimes does not. Women in general have sought emotional orgasms, peaks of love, far more than great physical orgasms. It seems likely that men too are searching for those experiences that melt the heart. A physical orgasm, whether genitally localized or enjoyed more generally throughout the body, is only as moving as the feelings accompanying it. When the heart has an "orgasm," when it melts in the ecstasy of love and the fullness of tender feelings, this is a truly unforgettable experience. And while the sensation of physical orgasm leaves the body within seconds, the feelings of the emotional orgasm are often maintained at a delicate level of pleasure to be enjoyed in waves of love again and again with a look or a smile.

Because they have had much more experience with non-orgasmic or non-goal-oriented sex, it is likely that women are more experienced in the level of lovemaking that has been called "transcendent" sex or "unboundedness" occurring during sexual activity. Without orgasm, sexuality has the opportunity to become diffused into a more subtle exchange of energy and love. And women who have experienced this kind of sexuality are actually enjoying a level of experience which has been generally reserved for the practitioners of the highest art of lovemaking in many cultures. But a woman (or a man) can only experience this kind of diffused expansion if she (or he) is not misled into thinking that only sex with orgasm quickly achieved is valid lovemaking.

The Sexuality of the Older Woman

According to Wade, Seaman, and others, most women tend to have increased sexual desires after the age of thirty. This eroticism is said to increase and continue through menopause and after, until about age sixty-five, when a slow decline in sexual interest begins. Dr. Helen Kaplan explains: "While some women report a decrease in sexual desire, many women actually feel an increase in erotic appetite during the menopausal years.... From a purely physiologic standpoint, libido should theoretically increase at menopause, because the action of woman's androgens...is now unopposed by estrogen."[8]

Dr. Mary Jane Sherfey also found that women become more sexual as they get older, perhaps because of the development of a larger system of veins in the genital area. So it seems that although older women are not capable of reproductive sex, they are more capable than ever of experiencing sexual pleasure. Shere Hite writes that women should think of their bodies as sexually capable for a lifetime but with reproductive capacities limited to a certain number of years in the middle.

As one older woman reported to Hite: "I think that men are conned into believing that [sex] decreases in age for them. I don't think it decreases drastically for anyone, especially for women. My best sexual experiences are coming out of maturity and self-confidence."

Given the fact that older women are sexual women and, like men, have the ability to be sexual all their lives, a similar confusion has developed. Like older men, older women in our society are put in a most difficult situation that demands an impossible integration of physical and social requirements. On the one hand, women are exploding the myth that older women are not sexual by continuing their sexual lives well into their seventies and eighties. On the other hand, women are beginning to feel a certain social obligation to be sexual at a time in their lives when other kinds of experiences may fascinate them more. Formerly, the social pressure to maintain sexual activity in their later years was less of a problem for women than for men, primarily because for so many hundreds of years, older women's sexuality was not welcomed. But that has changed.

Ironically, in an effort to be fair to older women, writers like Hite seem to put more pressure on older women to be sexually liberated than they do on younger women. But it seems that the dignity and level of experience of age should permit both older women and older men to be at last free of the narrowness of sexually oriented social acceptance.

Older women have the option to be sexual or celibate, based not on what they "should" be having in the way of sexual lives, but on their actual interest. For, given the physical possibilities, any woman can have sex at any age, but not all women want to. A woman may feel she needs to continue to prove her sexual attractiveness whether she wants sex or not, but this is a decision she must make. Not all women need that reassurance.

Many older women do not have the opportunity to be sexually involved, especially if they are divorced or widowed. To be put into the position of feeling deprived because they are not leading full sexual lives is a psychological burden most older women could do without. The real sense of worth and fulfillment can never come from sex anyway: the older woman misses the value of her development if she allows only her sexual life to represent her at age seventy. Sure, she has sexual feelings and desires—and so do five-year-old girls. But it is better not to mistake this one small avenue of self-expression for the power of womanhood at any age.

CELIBACY AND TODAY'S WOMEN

Temporary celibacy may be one of the healthiest choices a woman can ever make in her sexual life.
——BETTY HOLCOMB, "THE CASE FOR BEING CELIBATE"[9]

Throughout the ages, women were supposed to just say no. But then things changed. The good news was that women finally acknowledged their own sexual nature and began to enjoy themselves and be supported in this aspect of their lives. The bad news was the concurrent pressure to always say yes. As the eminent psychologist Rollo May wrote twenty years ago in *Love and Will*, "Where the Victorians didn't want anyone to know that he or she had sexual feelings, we are ashamed if we do not. . . . The Victorian nice man or woman was guilty if he or she did experience sex. Now we feel guilty if we don't."

Today, there is once again societal approval for saying no.

Health professionals are reporting an increase in the number of women choosing to be celibate today, not only because of the fear of AIDS, but because the desire for an integrated experience of a love relationship based on real friendship is far more compelling than the desire for a sexual caper. This is a dramatic shift in attitude over the last two decades, but not an unpredictable one.

According to Martha Allen, editor of the *Celibate Woman*

Journal, "Just hearing that celibacy is an option has a freeing effect on many women." Years ago, she notes, some women may have come to celibacy from a bad place, because of negative sexual and emotional experiences, but she now finds, judging by the essays and letters which arrive on her desk, that many women are currently choosing celibacy because of its positive value in their lives.

When asked to evaluate this choice in terms of reactions to the AIDS situation, Allen points out that celibacy is also a rising phenomenon among lesbians. Because lesbians as a group are least likely to become exposed to the AIDS virus (provided they are not intravenous drug users), the fact that there is an increase in the number of lesbians choosing celibacy is of importance in understanding the societal shift to celibacy apart from AIDS.

Allen reports a mixed reaction to this situation. A number of women, whether straight or gay, feel a certain amount of responsibility to retain the hard-earned sexual freedoms of the sixties and seventies against what they perceive to be an antifeminist, antigay backlash. But many reflective essays written by women who are choosing to be celibate despite this pressure indicate they are happier with and within themselves and seem to need less support for their choice. On the other hand, there *is* more societal support for their choice nowadays. And women are apparently glad to have it. A July 1988 survey conducted by *Cosmopolitan Magazine* reports a record number of "Cosmo" women aged nineteen to forty-five—women generally considered to represent a most liberated readership—opting for celibacy (9 percent). In addition, half the women surveyed had only one sex partner during 1987; one-third had only two; and only 8 percent had more than two lovers during the year. Overall, 68 percent of the women reported they are pleased with "the new (lack of) sexuality," finding it "a relief."

What is perhaps most surprising is that no one is really surprised. Just a few years ago in 1986, when columnist Ann Landers published similar results of her survey on women's physical needs, it caused a much bigger stir. Of the 90,000 women surveyed nationwide, 72 percent said they would prefer "being held close and treated tenderly" over having sexual intercourse. Of these women, 40 percent were under forty years old.

Valuing Celibacy

Most women are celibate or without sex for extensive periods of time in their lives—whether as a youngsters or as widows, as single women, divorcees, or even during marriage for a variety of reasons. But the tendency on the part of many women has been to disregard the growth experienced during these times and to consider only the times of sexuality to be valuable. It is safe to say that most women with a long history of confused sexuality would naturally be wary of any sign of the "re-repression" of their sexuality. What they fail to see is that at another level, being celibate by choice is more liberating than being sexual by demand.

Most studies on women report that as women finally become aware of their habit behaviors, dependencies, and low self-esteem, they begin to reject sexual relationships which are not valuable for them. They recognize how men and women can get into binding behaviors that are mutually restrictive. They seek to develop entirely new kinds of relationships based on less inhibiting ways of relating. For a number of women, celibacy offers that opportunity.

It is unfortunate that some women focus upon celibacy as a negative state of aloneness even among friends. It is also surprising to find that many offset their perception of the loneliness of celibacy with masturbation. The real benefits of celibacy do not happen when one is physically sexual and emotionally cut off.

Becoming celibate for a time is less a closing off than an opening up. It allows women to break old patterns of behavior, dependencies, limits. Women find that becoming celibate enables them to experience a greater degree of self-sufficiency and freedom while at the same time offers a chance to explore new dimensions in relationships. It can be a time to free a woman from the frantic nature of sexual activity and its narrow focus. And it can be a time to sort out feelings about a particular relationship without the mask of sex—to allow the deepening of a love relationship to occur in a more unbounded field.

Women who practice celibacy have experiences that range from their good feelings about finally "taking charge of their own bodies," to experiences of increased energy in all aspects of their lives, to feelings of peacefulness, settledness, "centeredness" and the development and growth of spiritual life.

The Effects of Celibacy on Women's Lives

When experienced at its best, women report that celibacy serves to expand their enjoyment of the sexuality/sensuality continuum. There is a more profound experience resulting from their commitment to celibacy than merely turning off to sex. As one woman has observed:

> Sexuality is but one facet in the spectrum of sensuality. When I read a poem and its metaphors paint a stark image, or if I latch onto a rhythmic cadence, my reaction is visceral. At times it is ecstatic; it is something I can "breathe" into my being mentally and physically. A musical chord can send shivers of delight up my spine. A pond can infuse me with rapture as I gaze on the play of sunlight on water. My *body* reacts. There is a complete communion with my environment—something that to me is at least as good and often better than sex. Like sex, these communions are intimate and intense. Unlike sex, they do not pose the scenario of two separate egos interacting: Spiritual sensuality is selfless, and selfless on many dimensions. When my

ego does come into play, it is myself whom I confront
rather than another person.[10]

Becoming Celibate

Writes Martha Allen, editor of the *Celibate Woman Journal:* "To
me an intimate relationship may or may not involve sex. For
the celibate individual it would not involve sex. What made
the celibate lifestyle a possibility for me was the realization
that it could include intimacy and affection but exclude the
focus on sex and genital preoccupation."[11]

Women who are experiencing a time of celibacy can choose
it either as a way to be alone and free of all relationships or as
a path to greater intimacy. Some celibate women find that not
worrying about sex opens them up emotionally with others
and that, interestingly, others are more open to them: "The
fear and insecurity often associated with ego is absent, more
so in men, in that they realize you don't see them as sexual
performers and so they tend to relax when in your company."
Another woman reports that celibacy helps to "spiritualize"
her life: "I find that in platonic relationships, my love and spiritual strength multiplies. On the other hand, when I am sexually involved with someone, my energies are drawn away
from my spiritual self."

Here are comments from a number of women who have
had periods of celibacy throughout their adult lives. In general, they tended to regard being celibate in a very positive
way—not as a social disability but as a time for improving relationships, a time to evaluate the role of sexuality and as a
means for personal independence.

"Because I need to feel a *real* commitment to a man in order to have an ongoing sexual relationship, I am currently
celibate. I used to have sex often, but I found that without
commitment, sex doesn't get any better than the first time
you have it with someone. The first time always seems the
best and after that, less and less of that anticipation and
openness is there—and then you spend later times trying to
recapture it."

"While I am celibate, I am able to experience my friends in the present—more for *all* of who they are than just a part of them. The intimacy is very deep when there is no goal like orgasm. My giving to them isn't held back for some future time when they 'deserve' it—like saving your energy for right before the finish line."

"It is a true test of men. If, when they find out I'm celibate, they don't immediately lose interest, then they're usually interested in meeting me in some more important place, and right away we've got more going for us than if we'd entered the first bedroom along the way."

"When I was celibate [last year], I found I had much more of *me* to invest in my work. At times, I felt less social than I do when I am not being celibate, but at other times I felt that my work was really more rewarding than any relationship I could have had at the time and that I was being really honest with myself to accept what other people saw as slightly 'wrong'—to be more interested in what I was doing on my job than in having a sexual/social life. I think many women committed to a career must go through this from time to time."

"Better than sex plus orgasm, I have always preferred to touch and be touched on a much more relaxed, unpressured basis, always staying in tune with myself throughout the physical exchange. So I am celibate most of the time and yet maintain an active 'touch' life when I can find people to appreciate that experience as much as I do. Actually, it was a man who taught me the value of touching. I'm not frustrated because I get a lot of emotional nourishment this way, and I save sex for the few people who really capture my heart."

"Interestingly, since I've been celibate, my sexual interest has stayed about the same, but I'm not at all frustrated in that I have the right to decide how to use the energy that sexuality enlivens in me. It's really a great resource."

"My views and opinions about life have changed drastically in my three years, plus, time of celibacy....I've had some surprising insights into sex, love, human nature in general. ...Do you want to know the degree of respect and empathy people in your life have?...Tell them you're celibate and their reaction will give you an immediate, close estimate of their intelligence and understanding of life."

"This may surprise you, but I like being celibate because I'm not wary about going out any more. *I* decide if I like a guy without sex confusing the issue. Before, even though I was never really hung up sexually, there was always this fear that I wouldn't measure up to a man's expectations of me sexually. This was most gruesome when I wouldn't even know the man, and I'd be getting ready to be 'judged' on my physical attributes by a total stranger. And you wonder why women who are so against beauty pageants and the like are willing to go through similar anguish. Now, I feel in control and happy with my self and, truthfully, a lot closer to men."

Celibacy as a Means to Sexual Liberation

As they have gained awareness of their own sexual independence, women are becoming aware that being sexually independent does not mean being independent from *people* but being independent from *sex*. Choosing to be with someone sexually means two things: (1) that one has chosen to be with that person and (2) that one has chosen to be sexual. Lovers don't limit women's fulfillment sexually—it is sex that is limited, far more so than being with another person with all other channels of communication beginning to open. It is clear to people who have experienced celibacy and continued to have relationships that these relationships expand immeasurably without the restrictive nature of socially defined sexual expression as the height of value in romantic relationships.

The kind of self-expansion and related social expansion which times of celibacy can bring come about through the softening effects of unrestricted love diffused throughout all experience. And celibacy for a woman is not good if it is not generous. It must not be repression or refusal but a natural coinciding of her behavior with the most loving dimensions of her nature to enable her to enjoy new horizons in her life.

FIVE CELIBATE WOMEN
INTERVIEWED IN 1979

Evie: Age Twenty-six, Dancer

"I have been celibate for about a year. My main reason for becoming celibate was that I wanted a way of really seeing where I was at with a man and where he was at with me. I have really wanted to be appreciated by men for the more sweet, giving, and innocent aspects of my being. If I go out with a man now, and he knows that I'm celibate, I assume that he is with me because he is interested in me not primarily as a sexual person but for other reasons. In the beginning, I remember thinking to myself, 'How many dates will it take until he loses interest?'

"I've always wanted to be more intimate in my relationships than the sexual kind of intimacy permits. The activity of sex does not seem to promote the kind of intimacy I am looking for. It's funny because I am actually very sexual, not at all asexual, but being celibate has given me a new way to investigate my feelings and to appreciate myself more. And my relations with men have deepened. I am not as anxious as I was when sex was *the* criterion for a successful relationship, and I feel a great deal more *myself*—like this is who I really am—I am not going to fool you with sex. I have met some truly affectionate men who make me feel very womanly and nurtured and appreciated even without the "reward" of sex. I love to touch and be touched and this has certainly not diminished but has become even more meaningful.

"In other aspects of my life, I notice a kind of strength, and I really think it's from being celibate even though I know that sounds quite medieval. In dance, I have more energy, and I am less fearful and uncertain. I feel like I have entered another dimension in my dancing coming from a sweeter, purer place in my heart.

"Preoccupation with sex has definitely diminished. I used

to think about it all the time. Even masturbation, something I never thought I'd ever want to stop, has somehow dropped off automatically.

"I think I'll be married one day, and when I am, I don't want to be celibate in the marriage unless it's totally natural for both of us. But I do see myself being comfortably celibate until I'm married or until I am with a man in a very complete way on all other levels."

Alexandra: Age Forty-two, Counselor

"I've been celibate for about four years. When I first thought of being celibate, I didn't even know the word 'celibacy.' I had been going out a lot, having sex, feeling drained, out-flowing, scattered, as though I were giving myself away. The physical acts of sex were fine, enjoyable, but I rarely felt energized from the experience.

"I have been married twice and was divorced five years ago from my second husband. We had a relatively good sex life, but once the orgasm was over, I always had an after-feeling of not being 'whole.' My lack of interest in sex was an issue in the marriage. It became a major issue at the time of divorce, but I think the real problems in our marriage were covered up by our focus on the sex issue.

"I don't think sex is good or bad. I think of sex as the frosting on the cake. You can have it or not. If you have a good cake, you don't need frosting. And sometimes frosting overpowers a good cake or is used to cover up a bad one.

"Sex has never been the part of my life that most intrigued me. But my sexuality has always been very prominent in my awareness. My sexual chronology started early. I began menstruating when I was eight—I haven't grown physically much since fifth grade. I started having sex with boys when I was a freshman in high school. But I spent the six years before going through my sexual growth pretty much alone and building up a lot of expectation and fantasy about sex. I would watch my body change and observe how I felt. Not surprisingly, my first sexual experiences were pretty disillusioning. But they got better, and I've enjoyed a very pleasurable sex life. But now I feel as though I've been through the entire cycle of sexuality already. And I definitely feel that to prolong my sexual life until I'm sixty or seventy would be an imposition on the rest of my life.

"Since I've become celibate, I *use* my sexual feelings instead of giving them away. I watch the feeling; I get into it. I love how I feel in this quiet way. I don't try to avoid feeling sexual—rather, I play with the feeling. But I don't let it control me. I really don't like being run by anything—I especially don't enjoy being manipulated by a physical feeling. Most people don't, but when they feel sexual, they let the feeling take over to the point where all they can do is try and get rid of it and aim for release. Where many seem to run away from their sexuality, I *feel* my sexual feelings without trying to quickly minimize them through having sex.

"I sometimes have visualized sex activity as a leak in my energy pipe. If you stop the drip, you get a continuous even flow of energy without diverting it into a wasteful stream. For this reason, I don't masturbate, because my energy feels too precious to me.

"As a counselor, I help people get in touch with their feelings and fully live their experiences. Far beyond sex, what people seem to need most is 'naked' *intimacy;* many people I see never really relate 'unclothed' with their guard down to anyone, not even to their spouses.

I never advise anyone to be celibate. Most people I counsel would need a much greater support system for being celibate than is currently available within our social structure. Also, I believe that a person has to be in touch with his or her sexuality and not be frightened of it or uncomfortable with it before becoming celibate. Otherwise, they may be very divided and feel unintegrated. I do have one friend who is also celibate, and we support each other in this.

"I've experienced some interesting benefits from celibacy. I lost forty pounds in the first six months. When actively sexual, I had experienced my body as round, from a constant search outward for nurturance through sex. On becoming celibate, I seemed to 'pull in' my energy; in turn, my body became stronger and more upright in my mind. The weight just dropped off. Another thing that happened is that I'm much more able to be physical with others. I'm much more present in the experience instead of waiting for the 'next step.' I feel less restricted, less threatened, more spontaneous.

"I feel more pure, more whole, more true to myself and much more able to love deeply. My sexual energy seems to flow easily into my feelings of love. I really enjoy giving to others because, unlike sex, it doesn't end and there is no need for a mutual payoff. I used to go outward with my energy both sexually and socially. Now I go inward, and I believe that is why my ability to love has deepened.

"Being celibate hasn't meant not being with men. Quite the contrary—I don't 'date' a lot, but I have a great many male friends, one in particular. Recently, after a movie, he brought me home, took me upstairs, undressed me, and gave me a full body massage. Afterward, he said, 'I feel closer to you now than if we had had sex together.' It was a very intimate expression of love for both of us.

"Almost everyone I know is sexually oriented, but most men seem to respect my desire to be celibate. I generally let them know if I'm asked out. They either don't mind, are intrigued, or feel challenged. If the latter happens, we go our separate ways.

"I think one has to be ready to be celibate just as one has to be ready to be sexual. But you have to be able to choose for yourself based on your own needs. I can't advise it for everyone."

Roxanne: Age Fifty-four, Fashion Coordinator

[Roxanne has been married three times since age twenty, has one daughter, and has been divorced for the past twelve years. She estimates that she has had seven affairs thus far in her life, only one since her last divorce.]

"My being celibate is a constant choice with every man I meet. I just couldn't hop into bed. I'm very choosy. I'm all for sex, but it's got to be part of a bigger thing. By itself, sex doesn't mean much. There's got to be a depth of relationship. I had one sexual affair since my last divorce. I thought it would be 'good for me'—that's what everyone says. But it didn't work. I have to have that deep involvement. So I'm celibate.

"I seem to be different from other women—particularly the younger ones who tend to treat sex more casually and more on its own. Celibacy partly represents my self-esteem, I guess; I'm celibate because I want more than sex, and I can't compromise. I think it's made me stronger.

"I have always enjoyed sex a great deal. It's very pleasurable. And I have a lot of sexual energy. So I've learned to use it in nonsexual ways. Rather than worrying about what to do about feeling sexual, I use my sexual energy to get things done. I look at it as a positive energy flow that's all mine. I can bring it to any part of my body; I use it in my arms and legs for running or lifting. I bring it to my mind for talking, for learning. So, for me, being celibate doesn't mean I'm blocking my sexuality. I use it and it keeps me strong, dynamic, youthful. I think sex keeps you young, but you don't have to express your sexuality in just one way. You can use it anyway you want. Many women my age are not that interested in sex, particularly in their marriages. It's become dull. But they feel they *should* be sexual, so they feel guilty unless they're 'with it.' They have sex, but they don't enjoy their sexuality. They perform, but they are blocked. I'm celibate, and I use and enjoy my sexuality without being blocked. It's a funny paradox.

"I'm an artist, and my creative growth is very important to me. I realize that the biggest periods of growth in my life have come during periods of celibacy. It's a very tangible growth which affects my daily living. As a woman alone, I supply my own needs. I have to draw love and affection from many sources. Without a deep relationship, I have learned to feel love through music, through the visual arts. I feel enlivened through a book, sharing ideas. It seems that as I've grown older, I've developed a level of deep awareness and love which must be touched for me to grow further. If I'm not deeply touched in a relationship, it's less satisfying than reading a book which truly moves me. I'm celibate because I look for *that* level in a relationship."

Sarah: Age Thirty-five, Professor of Language

"I have always enjoyed sex. I guess I am one of the minority of women who are so constructed that they can have orgasms during intercourse, and this has always been a great pleasure for me. I never realized how fortunate I was until all the information on women's sexuality came out. But because I've always found sexual pleasure to be an 'easy' experience for me (there wasn't much for me to learn or do better), sex has never provided much of an opportunity for growth in me. If you enjoy it a lot, you experience it fully, and then you begin to see its limitations.

"About two years ago, I made a conscious decision to be celibate. It seemed like a natural happening. I was finding that sex, although enjoyable, was binding. What I mean is that for sex to be meaningful, you have to have a commitment to your lover. If you are to be faithful, you are in a sense bound sexually to your lover. Bound in this way, you expect tremendous rewards for the boundary. Sex has to keep being great for you to keep being committed. That level of relating starts to dominate the relationship. Sex seems to keep you at one level of relating when you really feel like you want to soar with it. You get lost in the activity, and you end up being committed to sex rather than being committed to more freeing, more delicate, more subtle possibilities that you are yearning to experience.

"I love physical warmth and find it wonderfully nourishing. I find I am comfortable in a sensual, nonsexual relationship where I am not bowled over and I am not depending on sex to relate to the other person. If I lose myself, my 'center,' then I am not really enjoying the momentary experience. I discovered this in a particular relationship with a man I deeply loved. When I could take pleasure in each moment, each moment was a great thing, but with a focus on orgasm, the future became more important than the present.

"I also have found, by contrast to being celibate, that sex is fatiguing. I never really realized it, but I used to feel quite dull afterward and not very open to the person I was with. Being celibate offers all sorts of advantages—I relate more fully, more receptively, I am more alert and attuned; each moment has meaning. I feel stronger, more self-sufficient but also more open to loving and being loved deeply. It's actually more sensual being celibate than being sexual. Maybe I should write *Memoirs of the Sensual Celibate!"*

Marla: Age Twenty-four, Graphic Artist

[Marla was celibate for two years—from age twenty to twenty-two— following the death of her boyfriend. She is currently living with a man with whom she has a nearly celibate relationship.]

"I guess you could call me a child of the 'beat generation.' My father is a jazz musician, my mother is a writer and has been a practicing Zen Buddhist for twenty-five years. My parents met in Paris in the fifties. But when I came along, I think they became more conservative. I was educated at Catholic parochial schools. I spent a good part of my teen years reading romantic novels. My parents never told me the 'facts of life': I guess they assumed I already knew them. My education came out of these novels and from my peers, and I always knew I wanted to 'save myself for love.'

"What I thought was love came when I was fifteen: I had my first sexual experiences, but they were not at all what I had expected from the romances. In fact, they were pretty boring and unappealing—very different from my fantasies.

"When I was seventeen, I met Bill. He didn't talk much— he was very intuitive and perceptive. He also had great stability, love, and contentment with life. He really opened up my emotions and my sexuality. We lived together for a year and a half and then he was killed in an accident.

"After the initial shock wore off, with friends and family helping, I became quite reclusive. The expression 'she grew up fast' applied to me. Sex became a very serious issue for me. I resolved to take it seriously because I felt that the kind of sexual experiences I wanted would have to come from a really deep love. I guess it might have been a kind of vow somehow to make up for the loss of Bill. But it wasn't difficult for me to be celibate; it was the only way I felt. I didn't feel depressed; I just felt inward.

"I became a more serious person all around. This is when my work became very enjoyable and productive. I finished my degree in art and even had a successful exhibition of my drawings.

"The longings I had were not sexual—they were on a more heartful level. The needs I felt were for tenderness and someone to hold me. Even though everyone around me was very concerned with sex, my attention just wasn't on it. I felt it was a waste of time, and I saw how convoluted it had become. Most of my friends were older than me, but I felt older than them. I was lonely, but I was also aware of wanting to be alone.

"I started working in L.A. as a graphic designer. I began to feel more open to being involved with a man. I remember thinking, 'I'm ready.'

"When I met Roy, it was the first time in two years that I thought someone was even attractive. Neither one of us had had even a dating relationship for a long time, and we both had been celibate—he for a year, and I for two. Naturally, we were both shy and cautious, but in a week we knew that we were going to be together—even sexually.

"Initially, we were very conscious of having sex—it was really intense. I was scared but excited—it was not at all casual. We were very respectful of our sexuality. After all, we had 'saved it up,' so to speak. And it was great at first—a very spiritual exchange. But what I found was that as we began to have more and more sexual experiences together, we stopped communicating in other ways. We kind of let our minds go and became noticeably less interesting, at least intellectually. It was like giving each other a sexual gift was all we had the energy to give. Sex inspires you to give your all. But you don't always feel like giving more.

"It has become a funny kind of dichotomy between our minds and our bodies. Either our bodies *or* our minds are joined, but rarely both at once. I have found that when we have sex, it's usually when we haven't been as emotionally together. When we feel we are really joined, it's a level of intensity that's difficult to maintain, and sex always overpowers that feeling. If we have to be celibate in order to maintain that intensity, it's no sacrifice.

"Nowadays we are celibate most of the time and perhaps have sex once a month. It's a very good balance for us, and I prefer the results in all the other aspects of our relationship."

Celibacy in Marriage
Chastity Begins at Home

6 One is not born to be married: marriage is, as they say, an "acquired taste." One learns how to be married by being married, by observing one's parents, by having marriage-like experiences before marriage or instead of marriage. And how we value marriage will depend on how we learn to be married. The mutual learning that occurs in marital relations and the levels of intimacy derived from that learning form the basis on which a marriage grows.

Much of the marital focus of the past decades has been on the growth in sexual knowledge that has taken place in premarital and marital relations with regard to mutual needs and practices. A number of researchers have pointed out that men and women are very different in their sexuality, due in part to the different ways they experience sexual learning.

Learning to give pleasure to one's spouse thus requires an understanding of his or her needs and capabilities; this has been the value of the information revolution in sexuality. This knowledge has helped to prepare couples who may not otherwise have realized the differences in sexuality between men and women. On the surface, therefore, it would seem that the sexual revolution mainly brought about the learning opportunity for more and better experiences in marriage. But in reality that sexual emphasis in marriage created a more narrow and restrictive evaluation of marital success—one based almost entirely on sexual success. And as a possible consequence we began to see a rapidly growing dissolution of marriage and family life.

In the seventies and mideighties, nearly one in two marriages were ending in divorce. While we cannot blame "too much sex" alone for this complex phenomenon, still we cannot help observing that this divorce rate came about as sexual satisfaction became more and more valued, more valued than any other criterion of "good" social behavior—including other aspects of marital satisfaction. And so, when we did not find sex up to newly acquired expectations within the structure of marriage, we looked somewhere else—in some other relationship or social situation. And in this way marriage was sometimes regarded as an imposition or barrier to personal happiness, especially if that happiness was thought to be primarily gained through sexual activity.

Today, as we are again becoming monogamous as a society, with the divorce rate now falling, it is even more crucial to rethink the role of sex in marriage to avoid unnecessary and false expectations.

SEX AS THE MIRROR OF MARRIAGE

Most people realize that it is the quality of the love relationship that determines the quality of the sexual relationship, not the other way around. Yet this obvious understanding is often lost in the current overemphasis on sexual living.

It may be fair to say that in recent years there has been no greater pressure in a marriage than sexual performance. Sex has become the mirror of marriage. If their "sex life" is not experienced as profoundly fulfilling, a couple is taught to recognize that their marriage is failing.

As a result, some marriages are almost entirely sexually

dependent; the partners use sex as the exclusive path for their expression of intimacy and their continued willingness to share their lives. Many of these couples also use sex to control each other—demanding sex as a service, giving it as a reward, or withholding it as a punishment. These sex-based marriages are very difficult to maintain, as one or both partners are often unable to sustain sexual interest intense enough to uphold the whole marriage.

Even in more balanced marriages where the focus is not so one-sided, the sexual concerns are often used as a psychological filter for all the marital concerns. In his study of modern sexuality commissioned by *Playboy*, Morton Hunt concluded that a marriage is going well if "the sex" is good. Then, he reasons, there is not much need for extramarital sex, and the couple can remain faithful to one another.

Sex is even used to qualify emotional success in marriage. Women who do not have orgasms during sex with their husbands view their husbands as undependable and have been found to have a greater fear of losing them than "sexually successful" women. Masters and Johnson have noted that almost all the marriage guides available center their guidance on the premise that sex is the best indicator of success or failure in a marriage. Thus, as H. J. Campbell observed, "The fact that sexual joy is supposed to be an unquestioned feature of successful marriage will inevitably cause each partner to consider the marriage void for this reason alone."

In the early part of this century, Dr. Arthur Gould wrote that *over*indulgence in sex is "without doubt the cause of more unhappy marriages than any other influence. . . . It is the very fact that before marriage these fluids were retained in the body that created the magnetism which made the man and the woman so attractive to each other." Without defending or arguing against the validity of this view, we can at least appreciate the fact that not so many years later, the opposite theory for marital discord is now widely upheld in our society. Without an abundance of high-quality sex, a marriage may be viewed as a failure or empty of meaning. *Under*indulgence in sex, therefore, is considered to be the reflection of an unhappy marriage.

P.S.: Your Marriage Is Failing

Steve, thirty-three, has been returning home after work each evening full of excitement about his current project. He is finally getting to write—a long-held desire he never thought would be fulfilled at work. The boss likes his style and wants to give more writing responsibilities to him. Steve's whole attention is with his new assignment; he takes pleasure in his work. As he polishes each sentence, his mind and creative juices become absorbed in the task.

The last thing on Steve's mind these days is sex.

Steve's wife, Mary, also thirty-three, has been doing a lot of reading lately. After work, she has returned home to the books on sex with all the latest research and teachings. Encouraged by what she has read, she has been doing some of the exercises and has discovered a great thing—her unlimited capacity for orgasm. Mary is thrilled and eager to share and explore this new dimension of her physical life with Steve, who has always been the more sexual of the two. Mary takes Steve's lack of interest in sex as a sure sign that their marriage is falling apart.

In an article entitled "Making Love: The Subtle Art of Matching Moods," Marcia Lasswell and Norman Lobsenz described the impossibility of finding perfection in the sexual encounter every time and how continued disappointments lead to eventual lack of sexual interest on the part of one or both partners. They reported that therapists see more and more couples who are disappointed with their sexual lives together—not so much disappointed in the actual lovemaking as in the lack of mutuality of interests and times of being "in the mood." Most couples were found to have high sexual expectations and were not interested in casual sex even within marriage.

To combat the possibility that their marriage is losing its sexual definition, some couples go to the extreme of sexual appointments on a regular basis. Lasswell and Lobsenz noted that couples who use a schedule to make "reservations" in advance are faced with a problem of "too high expectations." In other words, sexual experiences do not seem to be altogether fulfilling when couples expect to have them regularly. That is because they are verging on becoming "habits."

Habits tend to be repetitive and contrary to growth. Habits, as routine behaviors in relationships, have been found to reduce the expansive nature of love and render its growth inconsequential. If sex becomes a habit, it tends to lose its spontaneity and becomes not only routine but negative. If a couple says, "We have sex every Thursday and Saturday," it is likely they have managed to routinize sex into a pattern not unlike the routine of housework. Sex out of habit performs a service and "sex-as-service rarely leads to sustained pleasure," observe Masters and Johnson.

Most married couples who feel that sexuality is a required part of marriage do get into a routine of sex, whether they want to or not. And that routine itself tends to make sex somewhat static or fixed or what Masters and Johnson call "goal-oriented." What is needed is the understanding that marital sex changes and cannot remain static if it is to be rewarding.

The basic kind of change in sexuality that will occur from time to time in a marriage is that one or both partners will become either more or less sexual. Over the past twenty years, the societal emphasis on sexuality created a sexual bias that favored the *increase* in sexual activity in a marriage and, therefore, often condoned looking outside the marriage for sexual satisfaction if just one partner seemed to require it. If one or both partners became *less* sexually interested, this was not so well regarded and may have been grounds for divorce.

But actually, the change toward lessening sexual activity may be indicative not of the failure of a marriage but of a higher-level relationship between the marital partners. It has been found that in the most successful, committed marriages, sexual response may indeed diminish in its localized expression—while changing into another kind of response.

Sexuality naturally changes in marriage over the months and years. And the change most frequently observed is the growth from a localized response to a more generalized response. As Masters and Johnson suggest, "Sex in a warm, emotionally-committed relationship may change in character and sexual response may become diffused after a while."

It is this *diffusion* of sexual response that many couples mistake for the *absence* of sexual response. And they begin to become very concerned that their marriage is losing its sexual orientation and, therefore, its value. What they may fail to recognize is that the essential direction of the growth of love generally progresses from the sexual experience to the higher expressions of love—that, in fact, as the sexual response in marriage becomes diffused, the opportunity for intimate love increases. As Dr. Helen Colton noted in *Sex after the Sexual Revolution*, "What is truly love may not even *begin* until that [sexual] tension abates."

As a marriage progresses and sexual experience and response change, it may be that one partner changes before the other. In the best marriages, these changes will be taken in stride by both, but if the changes are not acceptable to the other partner who is unprepared for a breaking down of the routine or an expansion of the boundaries, then a large communication gap will undoubtedly arise.

Is Sex Necessary for Marital Love?

Despite their mutual procreative function, sex and marriage are necessarily separate experiences and separate commitments. As behaviorist Campbell reminds us, "Sex is not inextricably involved with marriage or any other social institution. It is simply a form of sensory pleasure-seeking." And in its separate status, sex is a voluntary act and remains voluntary even within marriage. This voluntary nature of sexual activity in humans is what changes the sexual experience from the purely physical to the symbolic or spiritual union. Every sexual act within marriage is thus freely chosen—not automatically experienced unconsciously out of habit but consciously chosen out of love. And if a couple chooses not to express their love sexually, because sexual expression is not interesting to them at a particular time, their decision can only favor their freedom to choose wisely for themselves in their desire to enhance the growth of love.

A number of researchers have asked: *Is* sex a crucial feature of marriage? Does a healthy marriage necessitate an ongoing sexual relationship? No, not necessarily. Lewis Terman, a pioneer in the study of marital happiness, concludes: "Our data do not confirm the view so often heard that the key to happiness in marriage is nearly always to be found in sexual compatibility." At the University of Pittsburgh, in a study of happy marriages, two marital therapists found that more than 90 percent of their respondents had a "less than perfect" sexual relationship, but very few thought it was a problem in their marriages. One-third of the women questioned were more or less uninterested in sex but still felt love for their husbands. Forty-seven percent of the couples had sexual intercourse on the average between two and four times a month; 8 percent reported having intercourse less than once a month, and 2 percent had no intercourse at all. The study concluded that sex is not a crucial part of a happy marriage.[1]

In their comprehensive study of American couples, Philip Blumstein and Pepper Schwartz found that "a good sex life is central to a good overall relationship," but at the same time they concluded that, "many couples in long-term relationships are quite satisfied with sex lives that could be considered only moderately active." They point out that the institution of marriage supports a sexual bond but also can "preserve a married couple's relationship when the sex occurs infrequently." They further found, however, that unmarried couples, or "cohabitors," place far more importance on the sexual bond and, "if the frequency [of sex] is low, the relationship is bound to incur dissension." On the other hand, they noted that long-term, committed homosexual relationships, particularly between women, "can last even when the partners do not have sex very often." Such couples come to place the importance of a compatible partner above the sexual.[2]

In *The Mirages of Marriage*, William Lederer and Don Jackson report that "there is considerable evidence that an individual's *perception* of the sexual relationship is more related to marital satisfaction than the sexual act itself." They contend that frustration from the lack of sex "stems more from a feeling of deprivation than from pure physical necessity," that men and women can "live without sex and still stay healthy," as long as "the renunciation corresponds to [their] emotional needs." They found that within a marriage, a couple who have satisfying and happy sexual experiences may well have sex *less* frequently than "an unhappy pair frantically experimenting for a solution to their discord" and conclude that sex is in no way essential for a successful marriage.

In the face of the social pressure to define successful marriage based on sexual criteria, it is somewhat surprising to find that there is evidence pointing to the understanding that sex is *not* a requirement for a good marriage. What, then, has been the result of the sexual revolution in marriage? Superficially, it appeared to free couples to enjoy *more* sex, but in fact, if one probes deeper, it may be found that the sexual revolution may have, in effect, made sex *less* important in marriage than before.

The Demystification of Sex

We can regard the effects of the revolution in sexual knowledge as providing a concrete reduction in sexual mystification. Once sex has been demystified—known for what it *really* is and the specifics of its boundaries—a couple is free to experience the fullest nature of sex without the restraints of ignorance. Then, if they see that they want something more than sex can provide, they may move beyond those boundaries spontaneously. If we think that we're missing something, that something takes on a great importance, but once its value is known, it no longer holds such hidden fascination. Thus, in one sense, being free to be completely sexual together enables a couple to be free *from* sexuality so they may explore further horizons of the love relationship.

Most married couples have been taught that bringing sexual "fulfillment" to their partner is the most intimate contribution they could make to the marriage. But they also learn that the sexual aspect of love is limited; they know from experience that the best of all possible orgasms does not bring about fulfillment five minutes later. Some then come to see sex with a more balanced eye—as a form of play and pleasure but not as *the* basis for development in marriage. And then they may begin to build a more valid and more lasting foundation for a successful marriage.

In this search for ways to achieve marital growth, some couples are turning to celibacy in order to be entirely free of the sexual focus. In turning their sexual freedom around 180 degrees to celibacy, they are seeking to establish an entirely different basis for marital happiness and love. Celibacy can enable them to explore more deeply what they have together without the domination of sex. In this way, celibacy is a means to bring out and acknowledge the hidden values of marital love.

CELIBACY IN MARRIAGE

Celibacy or continence is presumed healthy for priests and nuns, the unmarried, children, the elderly, those institutionalized, and members of the armed forces away from home, but it is considered unhealthy for married adults.

——JOEL FORT, M.D.

It does not follow that the celibate and the couple are, as people think, in an opposite sexual situation. For both, continence is necessary. For the celibate, it is not only a matter of doing nothing. It is a matter of knowing oneself to be fully a man or fully a woman having social relations with men and women. Chastity alone makes this possible by triumphing over the temptation to limit one's concept of sex to sexual desire. . . . Man and woman form a couple. This is the conjugal love of which the genital aspect is only one necessary consequence.

———PAUL CHAUCARD

Without chastity, it is impossible to maintain the dignity of sexual love.

———HAVELOCK ELLIS

Perhaps Mary and Joseph were the most well-known celibate couple. George Bernard Shaw and Charlotte Payne-Townsend could be the next best known. They even signed a contract to maintain celibacy throughout their marriage.

But you generally don't hear too much about celibate marriage. (In fact, *celibate* is derived from *caelebs*, which means "single.") The idea that celibacy can be practiced during marriage may be as strange a concept to some people as the idea that priests can be sexual is to others. The traditional separation between celibacy and marriage is as strong as the traditional separation between sexuality and the priesthood. This would not be of much concern except for the unfortunate conclusion that spiritual development is associated with celibacy and not with sexuality. So marriage, in its commitment to procreation, has been aligned with sexual-nonspiritual life, and the possibility of spiritual development is "saved" for single people—and generally only those committed to a religious vocation.*

———

*One noteworthy opponent of this predominant view was Henry David Thoreau, who considered marriage only worthwhile in the most rarefied form of spiritual love. He wrote: "If it is the result of a pure love, there can be nothing sensual in marriage. Chastity is something positive, not negative. It is the virtue of the married especially. All lusts or base pleasures must give way to loftier delights."

Whereas love has been granted a spiritual component throughout history, especially by the poets, musicians, and artists, marriage has tended to be viewed as a more mundane affair, filled with worldly responsibilities and not really offering a good opportunity for higher spiritual development. And indeed, throughout most of history, marriage was based on economic and social considerations and had little to do with romantic love relationships, which were considered separate from marriage. Love and romance, as the basis for forming a marriage, were to come much later in the West and in some cultures have never been part of the experience of marriage.

Love and Marriage: A Recent Event

Love and aversion both wear off in matrimony, so that
it is better to begin with a little aversion.
——RICHARD SHERIDAN

Our concept that "love and marriage go together like a horse and carriage" is a relatively modern concept and is primarily a Western innovation dating from the time of the French Revolution. As odd as it may seem to us now, the idea that marriage could be the outcome of romantic love did not arise in our own culture until less than a hundred years ago. Marriage as a social merger based on economics, social status, family needs, and the like has always taken precedence over romantic love, even when great pain was inflicted on countless romantic lovers as the result of forced separation.

So love-and-romance marriage, although a testimony to the openness of a society willing to support a nonmaterial basis for a traditionally social enterprise, has not always been regarded as the most successful formula for marital life.

Even the open-minded Bertrand Russell, like many before him, saw marriage as a means to fulfill a social purpose based on "affection and realism," not on romantic response. Sixty years ago he noted: "In America, where the romantic view of marriage has been taken more seriously than anywhere else

...the result has been an extreme prevalence of divorce and an extreme rarity of happy marriages."[3]

In our society, we tend to consider romantic love a more valid or at least a more civilized reason to be married than if the marriage is "arranged." Yet such a basis for marriage does not seem to bring about lasting enjoyment or commitment. As Haich notes, "We are driven to the somewhat curious conclusion that the more civilized people become, the less capable they seem of lifelong happiness with one partner."

It may be that romantic love is not offering married couples a strong enough basis for a continuing commitment of growth in marriage primarily because the spiritual content of love has been kept separate from the usual commitments of marriage.

Today, when marriage is supposed to be based on a contract of love, it is still not understood as a channel for spiritual growth, and the historic distinction (in the West) between sexuality and spirituality still reinforces a primarily nonspiritual attitude toward marriage. But if the spiritual dimensions of love were added to the social-material enterprise of marriage, then hopefully all aspects could flourish.

Spiritualizing Marriage through Celibacy

Celibacy can be regarded as a way to "spiritualize" sexuality in order to refine the experience of love further. When a couple feels deeply connected and chooses not to express their love sexually, other ways to express those feelings start to emerge. When people are used to expressing love in the same way over and over, its expression is eventually reduced to just one channel, to one habit. But if love is redirected away from its usual channel, it finds new and perhaps more growth-producing channels in which to flow.

In this way, celibacy provides married couples with more choices of expression—a kind of limitless market of possible connections. It may be like "courting" all over again, but without the fear of rejection or the limitations of future goals. If a husband or wife brings flowers to his or her spouse as a first step or prelude to a great night of sexual love, the meaning of the flowers becomes lost in the chain of events that follow. But flowers in times of celibacy are a thing in themselves— perhaps the whole expression of love for that day—not simply an offering to ensure the future.

All the ordinary activities of a shared life may in fact take on new meaning and have greater value for a celibate couple. Without the old pathways of sexual exchange to rely on, love seeks and finds other levels of exchange. And these may, in turn, provide increasingly more unbounded, more refined, more fulfilling experiences in the marriage.

When certain associations stemming from the past personal histories of individuals have linked sexual activity with the restrictive qualities of dominance, control, bribery, "scoring," and other negative characteristics such as anger, resentment, jealousy, possessiveness, and emotional separation from sex, sexual love is at its least expressive level of fulfillment and may cause only unhappiness for a couple. To break the unfortunate patterns of association which have set in, celibacy can be used to enable love to be reexperienced at a simpler level of feeling.

Celibacy can give the couple the chance both to reestablish presexual communication of tender feelings and to open new channels of expression free from restrictive associative behavior. It can be a time for the renewal of old feelings that occurred before sexual habits set in, and it can be a time to discover other modalities of loving. It can re-create and create the unbounded qualities of romance—the intensity, energy, sweetness, and careful attention of two people falling in love.

An interesting phenomenon that happens in marriage is the uniting of the physical lives of the two. Happily married couples are often thought to look alike after a number of years—even if they started out looking very different from each other—as if they had exchanged some features and grown together physically. One view of why this happens is the idea that the nervous systems of the two actually begin to interconnect through an exchange of energy. The exchange begins initially on the level of sexual expression and continues to gr / in more subtle and more powerful ways over time.

If sexual interests start to fall away during marriage, it may be because the physical union of the couple is already operating in a continuous shared flow of energy in all marital activity. Some couples feel a continual outpouring and intaking of love and energy, particularly when a profound basis of trust and devotion has founded the kind of open receptivity needed for such an exchange. So the uniting of the physical ties that one yearns for in sexual union is already occurring, and sexual activity may be experienced as unnecessary or even undesirable—as a breaking of the flow, providing a less refined expression of an experience that is happening at more delicate levels of the physical nervous system. This more subtle exchange is experienced in feeling and thought—"being on the same wave length"—in the exchange of looks, hugs, and the energy felt sharing the same environment, the outer environment reflecting the inner.

This growth from expressed sexual union to a perhaps more intimate physical union is a common experience of marriage and long-term relationships, but one our society tends to overlook in the face of the popular, if misguided, desire to hold on to concrete sexual activity as the most significant expression of marital union. But when a couple has the chance to enjoy what they share at these deeper levels, without feeling concern about keeping old sexual habits maintained as *the* proper procedure of union, they may realize that they are experiencing a fuller range of love, a richer emotional and spiritual bonding together. This does not mean that sexual expression is forever eliminated: it merely allows what may be a natural kind of evolution to occur, and the sexual may continue to be enjoyed but in a less important role in the achievement of the physical aspect of marital union.

This phenomenon is most clearly understood if we consider, as we will in the following chapter, how sexual energy is transformed spontaneously into other kinds of energy in human development: how all the energy may be really the same but expressed in different ways according to the level of consciousness of the individual expressing it at any given time in his or her life.

Some couples adopt a celibate lifestyle as a way of relating from a comfortable and, according to them, physiologically natural place. Writes one 66-year-old great grandmother who has been married to the same man for forty-seven years and has enjoyed eleven years of celibate marriage:

> What of those who have enjoyed sex and borne children? Is there not a cycle for the ending of sexual activity as there is for the beginning? I am aware that most doctors, psychologists, psychiatrists and specialists in human behavior assure one and all that sexual activity should last through old age and even unto death. "Balderdash," say I.
>
> There is a cycle for sex as for every age. Around age 55, there is a lessening urge, sign of a new cycle, the freedom from sex if one will accept the freedom. This is the joy of celibacy. There are other things to do, to think about. Continued and compulsive sex will not change the cycle, will only lead to frustration and despondency.... Cycles have been observed from the beginning. The cycles of the moon affect the tides and our menstrual cycles.... The sun, moon and planets have been placed in the heavens that we may apply their cycles to our lives.[4]

Experiences of Marital Celibacy

One aspect of celibacy in marriage that can occur is nonmutual celibacy, where one partner becomes celibate but the other doesn't. Just as sexual interest in marriage can grow more intense in one partner than in the other, so can the desire to be celibate. But it is incumbent upon the partner who is undergoing the change in desire or behavior to be responsive to the feelings of the other.

If one partner wants to become more sexually active, it is usually because he or she feels unfulfilled sexually, which sometimes can be a focus for a more generalized lack of fulfillment. This situation is not uncommon in marriage; solutions dealing with it are suggested in numerous books on sexual relations. But if one partner wants to become celibate (and this could also be a common experience), there may be some confusion as to how to evaluate that desire in the context of marriage.

Essentially, it must be determined if the desire is due to a negative or a positive motive. In marriage, if one withholds sexual activity for negative reasons—to punish, control, or withdraw love—it is obviously not celibate behavior that can benefit a marriage. Going "on strike" against sex as the result of some argument or some temporary negativity is also not a useful assumption of celibacy. How then does a couple know if the desire to be celibate is positive?

Celibacy in marriage does not come about all of a sudden. If it does, it is suspect.

The growth toward celibacy, if it occurs at all in marriage, has been found to be a natural progression over time, not an immediate decision.

This point cannot be too greatly emphasized. Celibacy in marriage should only be practiced if it is comfortable for both partners and has been arrived at in a natural way. If one partner wants to be celibate but the other does not, the situation could create a major difficulty that can only be worked out in favor of the most sincere desire of both partners to further the growth of their love and commitment. If one can convince the other that a fuller experience of love lies ahead, the decision to be sexual or celibate will be based on that goal of increased happiness. Celibacy or sexual activity chosen *in the service of love* is the context in which a couple makes its decision.

How Long to Be Celibate?

Another consideration of marital celibacy is the issue of time. It doesn't matter how long a couple continues to be celibate if the situation remains progressive and comfortable. Some couples are celibate for many years, either in the later years of marriage—when sex no longer holds its former fascination yet love continues to grow—or sometimes in the early years, when a couple may be seeking to establish the most intimate pathways for their love to flow beyond the limits of sexual expression. Other couples are celibate for a month or two—which may offer the chance for sexual activity to rest and to be renewed at a deeper level of settledness and for patterns of exchange to be restructured beyond the insistence of habit.

By the same token, a couple would want to avoid getting into a habit of being celibate if the enjoyment of the growth of love had ceased. If celibacy occurred as the result of an overall lack of desire to be together or as a kind of withdrawal of mutual love and support, then it may be time to reexamine the motives for the lack of sexual activity. So the practice of marital celibacy and the length of time a couple might wish to maintain it will be dependent upon the kind of growth experiences they are sharing and the fulfillment it brings to the marriage.

The commitment of marriage is to the other's growth in life as well as to one's own. These are the bonds of marriages and love. Bertrand Russell wrote: "Love must feel the ego of the beloved person as important as one's own ego, and must realize the other's wishes and desires as though they were one's own."

Once a couple is united in commitment to each other on the basis not of need but of the desire for the other's personal growth to fulfillment, marriage becomes an ideal avenue for social and spiritual development and accomplishment. The two unite, forming a base of strength and a deep channel of energy to give out to the world.

From this commitment, marriage becomes a medium of

service—to each partner from the other and from both partners to the society and to all humanity. Growth in devotion,
growth in surrender, and growth in outflowing love from an
increasingly fuller heart are the signs of progress.

To maintain and advance the growth and flow of love in
this ideal state of marital union, there have been couples in
both past and present who have found that being celibate from
time to time—even for a long period of time—provides certain profound benefits. Some decide to be celibate to achieve
the benefits of a fuller love; others become celibate and then
realize the benefits they have been experiencing through the
growth of love. In either situation it is the expansion of love
which is desired and created.

THREE CELIBATE COUPLES
Interviewed in 1979

The perspective of celibate marriage can perhaps best be described by those who practice it. What follows are interviews
with three married couples, with some additional history to
present the sequence of experiences that led to marital celibacy.

Tom and Diane

Both are twenty-eight—Tom is a medical student and Diane
runs her own greeting-card business. Tom and Diane have
been celibate for three and a half years, married for five years,
and have lived together on and off for over ten years. They
are an energetic, bright, humorous, and lovable couple who
have a great number of friends and who maintain close ties
with their families.

DIANE'S STORY: Diane grew up in a successful farm-
ing community in Illinois, the second of six children. Her father is a business consultant and her mother is in charge of
the family's farm operations. Diane is a very warm and at-

tractive woman. She describes her family as always very physically affectionate and open about sexual matters—where talk about sex was commonplace. She says that she has always been "a physical person" and that sex was "never a big deal for her"—she was comfortable with her sexuality from the beginning. During high school, she had several boyfriends and experienced a lot of physical relating. She would have slept with her boyfriend in her senior year but "there was never a really good opportunity."

When Diane went to college, she met Tom at a picnic in the first week of her freshman year. "On the surface," she remembers, "he was cool and tough, but I sensed his soft core. He seemed much more sophisticated than he really was." According to Diane, it was purely accidental that she was still a virgin when she met Tom, but he saw it as a symbol of the purity of her nature. "He didn't want to 'corrupt' me, but I knew we were going to be together sexually. In one sense, we slept together because it would have been too big a deal if we didn't."

They started living together despite some doubts, especially on Tom's part. They both acknowledged that they would be married one day, but that a lot of growth would have taken place. Tom would say "I know I'm going to marry you, but I just don't want to be with you right now." In the summers they would be apart. Diane would return to the family farm and spend time with the hometown boys. Her main attraction to these other men was physical, she remembers. She had five or six of these physical affairs but would always long for the deeper connection she had with Tom. Sex with Tom was a pleasurable, but not essential, part of the relationship. Diane realized even then that perhaps the sexual aspects were becoming to some extent minimized.

TOM'S STORY: Tom, a cherubic, funny and highly intelligent man, spent his first twelve years in the Midwest, and then moved with his family to Washington. His father is a doctor and his mother a teacher. He has one younger sister.

Tom recalls his early sexual life as "normal" but feels that perhaps he was "more sexually oriented than most kids" he knew.

In the eighth grade, Tom experienced his first orgasm with a girl and "connected sex and woman for the first time." At his school, he became part of a fast crowd. He learned that "sex is what you should always want if you're a real boy. In this pursuit, I was inevitably stopped in my quest by girls who knew how to defend themselves." By the eleventh grade, Tom had "done" it but had also by this time managed to separate sex and feelings "as the result of internalizing experiences of rejection." His rules became: (1) "Get it on" and (2) "Don't get hurt." "I knew I wanted sex," he recalls, "but I definitely protected myself from love." He convinced his girlfriends that they couldn't love him because he wouldn't love them. He slept with whomever he could—perhaps fifteen to twenty girls. He felt he had an image to uphold. "It would have been another moral plane for me at that time to have seen a girl and not have wanted to sleep with her."

Tom remembers having fun but being unable to let himself go. He was still eager to prove himself, but by the time he started college, he realized that he needed a more mature relationship based on feeling, even though "I still hadn't outgrown my Don Juanism."

When he met Diane at the beginning of his freshman year, her innocence dazzled him. "I didn't want to deceive her like I felt I had deceived all the girls in high school. I knew *here* was a girl I could really love who could help me to love her and the relationship will go beyond sex finally." They became "best friends"—a friendship of intimacy. They also slept together "primarily to release the sexual tension" between them, but it was difficult for Tom to reconcile sex and love and commitment. "I was nowhere near integrated enough to be with her, yet I knew I wanted to marry her. I told her everything I could think of to turn her away from me, including tales about the other girls I slept with. I did a lot of sexual fantasizing *except* about Diane."

"In some way, sex for me was associated with a lesser part

of my true self. I couldn't really express my best nature in it. Diane's more uninhibited sexuality was hard for me to deal with. I wanted her to reach into me and pull me out of myself. But when she was very physical, she would be lost from me in her orgasm, emotionally apart, and I would feel isolated. I'd be withdrawn inside myself, and she'd be having these ecstatic experiences."

What developed was that when Tom and Diane were not getting along, when they were not touching each other emotionally, they would reunite sexually: the physical would bring them together. But when they were open emotionally, then "sex was not as enjoyable." "I wanted us to be parallel in our sharing and not be overwhelmed by sex. Diane thought I wasn't attracted to her, but I longed so much for her on a deeper level that I couldn't express it sexually. It wasn't enough." They developed a more passive approach to sexuality which was less "violent, softer, and seemed more in tune with our sharing of feelings."

A year before the marriage, Tom underwent a lot of changes. He grew from feeling contained, where the thought of commitment to Diane "felt like being trapped" to feeling more and more open, free—a release of blocked feelings. At the same time, at the end of his senior year, he reconciled his behavior by accepting himself as a man who preferred to relate to his lover on other than a sexual basis. In this resolution, he felt a strengthening in his commitment to the marriage.

Diane and Tom were married after living together solidly for a year during which time they had sex together about twice a month. Once married, Tom really began to want to be celibate. "I felt I had to keep our relationship in a deeper state than the sexual. I wanted us to be celibate so I could relate to her without any of my trips."

Diane recalls that she eventually began to understand the extent of Tom's desires to be more integrated in his feelings. He in turn, she says, grew more loving, more expressive and more intimate in the sharing of his feelings with her, and she eventually overcame her fears that he wasn't really attracted to her. "The real attraction was very powerful." By the second year of marriage, they both agreed to be celibate on a semipermanent basis, but with the idea that they would see what would happen in the growth of their feelings.

Several years later, Tom and Diane are still celibate and able to look over the results.

Some Questions and Answers

What do you get out of being celibate?

DIANE: Now, being together is like making love all the time. That may sound absurd to other couples, but celibacy seems to keep our hearts open to each other. Sort of the way it feels when you first fall in love....It's similar to this article I read which said that people who got along best as friends had the least amount of sex in their relationships. That the negativity between people seemed to increase the desirability of sex.

When did you decide to be celibate?

TOM: We were already pretty much celibate when we decided to be celibate!

Do you have any sort of physical relationship?

DIANE: We always play together. And we sleep together. We cuddle, we kiss and hug a lot. It's very spontaneous, but we don't get aroused to the point of intense sexuality.
TOM: It's something of the comfortableness that comes after sex—with the tension gone and just pure enjoyment. Maybe you could call it "hindplay." I never used to enjoy touching after sex. It would feel too personal, too real—without a goal, like the goal of foreplay.

Are you sexually attracted to people outside the marriage?

TOM: When I see attractive women, it's not exactly nothing— I look, but it's an appreciation—almost an aesthetic experience. I once heard a guy say almost that exact same thing about his reaction to beautiful women and at the time, I thought it was bull, but now I know what he meant. The physical desire just doesn't take you over in that overwhelming way, and you can really fully experience the woman's beauty without wanting to "have" her.

DIANE: The thought of sex with anyone other than Tom doesn't appeal to me at all right now. And with Tom, it's grown into something else.

How do you experience your celibacy?

DIANE: It's a pure thing. We feel good in it—in its purity. The reward is the deep love we feel together.

Besides that feeling, what keeps you both being celibate?

TOM: I feel more comfortable, more in tune with myself being celibate. The supreme test for me would be if I could have sex and enjoy it and it equaled how I feel emotionally. It still feels less than full to me, and it doesn't express what I feel for Diane.

DIANE: At this point, it's a lot easier for me to not have sex than to pass up an ice-cream cone. Being in the habit of not having sex makes it a lot easier, and I'm very much in love with Tom in this way.

How about having children?

TOM: We'll probably have children at some point in the future. It will be an act of love to have a child—something divine.

Do your parents know you are celibate?

DIANE: My mother knows. At first she thought I was unhappy because we were celibate, but now she sees the positive strengths of our marriage, and she thinks it's good.

TOM: My parents would think it was the end of the world if they knew.

Does celibacy have a purpose for you?

DIANE: Celibacy lets us be spiritual together. When we have sex again, we want it to be an act of worship. We see sex as being transformed into a different kind of experience through celibacy—making our love stronger within each of us and then in each other.

[I was able to talk with Tom and Diane again in 1988. They are now in their late thirties and still celibate after thirteen years of marriage. They are seriously thinking of having children.]

What are the continuing benefits of celibacy for you?

TOM: It feels as if it creates great spiritual strength. Your energy is transformed and everything becomes more sensuous, more satisfying, and you experience a lot of inner joy. In truth, celibacy brings me to a place of pure bliss inside where I feel completely open.

Do you think you are growing more or less intimate by being celibate?

TOM: Intimacy is a very profound and subtle thing. Years ago, I couldn't be intimate. I felt I was forcing a role. Not having sex in a sense gave me the freedom *to* be intimate; I learned to become intimate from the inside out. Our relationship now is a profound friendship; very delicate, very sweet. We rarely get angry or hurt with each other and if we do, it washes over in minutes. It's at that level of unshakable intimacy.

How have you managed to want to be celibate all these years?

TOM: If there's a continuing intimate relationship with the person, you're always in touch, literally in touch. So there's so much feeling of love and support and care, there's no lack of fulfillment. The waves of love I feel for my wife are extremely available, tender and spiritual. I experience it as an enormous freedom and happiness inside. Our relationship is so huge—there's nothing that constricts it or overshadows it. It's from a being level of life, full and nourishing.

Do you always find it easy to be celibate?

TOM: The only real way to be celibate, I believe, is if it's a natural thing. I think your hormonal habits change. If you don't have the localized need, it's easy. In this way, celibacy is more a reflection of an entire way of perceiving the world, a level of consciousness. I can't entirely ignore the sexual messages around me, but I find I can comfortably shift my attention from a lower tug to something more full. But at this point, celibacy is so stable and natural for me, I rarely think about it.

Do you and Diane have any kind of physical relationship at all?

TOM: We always have had a very physical relationship. We touch all the time. We cuddle and kiss, but we avoid arousal. It's not that I can't get aroused; I just don't go to that point.

What do you remember your experience of sex to have been?

TOM: Well, I certainly enjoyed sex on a localized level. But I wasn't extremely natural in that activity in that I wasn't at all settled inside. I was controlling myself inside, holding back, isolating myself, even if my sexual partner was very open herself. I just couldn't surrender, so it wasn't an expansive experience. For me sex represented a kind of loss of self.

I don't believe I'm alone in this experience. Most adolescents and most adults, perhaps more men than women, are unable to surrender. Then boundaries get confused; attachments get formed; needs get exaggerated.

It's my belief that you're only ready to have sex when you no longer need it out of an involuntary place. When you can honestly and freely choose to have it and have it in its fullest, most spiritual sense.

Was it always easy for you to forego sex?

TOM: I certainly wasn't ready or willing to be celibate before my desires shifted. It would never have happened if I hadn't been oriented to living a spiritual life. Sex was supposed to be fulfilling, but it really wasn't. I knew I wasn't fulfilled but I was most definitely into sex. When I discovered a deeper and truer level of my own nature, I changed and I couldn't go back to being sexual in that unconnected way. The idea of getting horny and aroused didn't appeal to me after that.

Do you think your wife would have been celibate had you not wanted to be?

TOM: My wife had no boundaries with me sexually. She was so secure that it kind of amplified my own boundaries. No, I don't think she would have been celibate.

Diane, would you have been celibate had you married someone other than Tom?

DIANE: That's a difficult question to answer because I don't think I could have loved anyone the way I loved and still love Tom. I probably wouldn't have been celibate, but I honestly don't miss sex. I could be happy either way. It feels entirely natural, comfortable, and rewarding to me to be celibate. Once we made that decision, I haven't thought much about it, except occasionally during the first years.

Do you think women have an easier time with celibacy than men?

DIANE: I think men's physiology is more hair-trigger in this area. Maybe that's why it's more of an issue for men to be celibate. For myself, as a woman, I feel very fulfilled and I can't see that having sex would make me any happier.

I know you're thinking of having a baby sometime in the next year or two. Are you concerned that being sexual is again going to feel less than full for you?

TOM: Actually, no. In a way, I think this long period of celibacy will have prepared me to experience it in the spiritualized value that colors all other aspects of my life. It's also part of a continuum this way, not simply stopping to be celibate, but continuing to reflect the growth of my relationship with my wife and our mutual desire to have children. Celibacy has been a necessary step for me, but it isn't so important now.

DIANE: The big issue I've been focusing on is more, Are we ready to have children? rather than on, Are we ready to have sex? I don't think being sexual again will be a big deal one way or the other. I don't believe I've lost my sexual response. I think if I put my attention on my sexuality, I'll be very responsive.

Are you thinking of having sex to have children as something other than celibacy?

DIANE: Quite honestly, it feels like the same idea to have what you might call a kind of celibate sex for a purpose and you continue to maintain a definite outlook on sex for a spiritual union, not simply entertainment. Of course, this makes you very much aware that you really want to enjoy it in its fullest because it's for such a wonderful purpose.

Once again, let me ask as I did years ago, do your parents know you're celibate?

DIANE: Our fathers don't know; our mothers do. I have talked quite often with my mother about it. She feels it's entirely natural and fine for us. I think it's something that's developed in her own marriage. My parents have been getting closer and more intimate in recent years, and she's indicated that the sexual aspect of their relationship is minimal.

I know you feel very private about your lives. Why did you allow me to interview you today and in the past?

BOTH: We wanted to alert people who might want to be celibate to this possibility and to reassure those that are. They may think there's something wrong with them. We think there are probably many more celibate married couples than people realize. Married couples should feel as comfortable with celibacy as anyone.

Would you recommend celibacy to other married couples?

BOTH: No, not at all. We think it's different for different couples. In one couple, the energy flows one way; it may flow another way for another couple. And it has to happen at the right time. We had friends in college who said they were celibate and we thought that was pretty weird. We couldn't imagine at the time making that choice!

Peter and Anne

Peter and Anne have been married for eleven years and have been celibate for two years. They have two sons—the oldest (age sixteen) is from Anne's first marriage and the other was born nine years ago. Peter is a contractor and Anne is an interior designer. They live in Philadelphia, where they have a successful business redoing old houses and apartments. They are a witty, urbane couple—easy to be around—who seem to have a deep understanding between them and a mutual high regard. They say that they've "weathered the storms of marriage" and feel they have the right to decide the rules for themselves "but not for others."

ANNE'S STORY: Anne is a tall, strong, lively forty-year-old woman who grew up in Cincinnati in what she calls a "strict WASP home." Her father was a salesman and her mother raised the three girls, of whom Anne was the eldest.

Anne recalls very rare discussions about sex with her parents; she learned from her peers. Her first "celibate love affair" occurred when she was thirteen. "He came up to my shoulders. It was definitely True Love." During her high school years, Anne became part of a group "who turned out to be the fastest girls in the school." She became what she calls a "social deviant," at least in the eyes of her family. She began drinking and bringing her various drinking companions home with her. She wrecked her father's car and generally "enjoyed doing what I wasn't supposed to do." She had a few sexual experiences starting in her junior year, "but I didn't know what I was doing and I knew absolutely nothing about birth control." All in all, she says, "I think I got over that whole uptight upbringing I had in one wild year. But sex was really not much more than a lot of dirty jokes to me."

Once at college, Anne's behavior and outlook changed. She settled into her school activities gratefully. During her second year, she met Victor, her first husband-to-be. He was "handsome and romantic—right out of a picture book." They started going together and Anne observes that her "sex education really began with Victor at this time." They married when they graduated; Anne was twenty-two.

The romance carried Anne through several years of a rocky marriage and the realization that Victor was very unstable. Their time together was "a constant challenge." "We really lived in a fantasy. We prolonged the romance through a number of emotional tricks but we never really dealt with each other as people. After our son was born, I was forced to take a good look at what we were doing. I was definitely ready for a more honest and mature relationship, and it sent Victor right out the door. He wasn't prepared to make a commitment to a wife and family."

Alone with a year-old child, Anne started working out of her home. In time, she built up a successful decorator business in her community. She was happy and fulfilled at one level, "but I was always looking for someone to be with after the work day was finished, and I would feel a wave of loneliness. I never really longed for sex; I longed for someone to look at, talk to, and touch."

When Anne met Peter, "I knew he was someone extraordinary—a man who could see me as a person *and* who really could appreciate my womanliness. He wanted that part of me —the tenderness, gentleness, and passion—the part I didn't get to use in my business. Things between us grew slowly; I never felt rushed or that I had to prove myself quickly to him before he found someone else."

"We were together for almost two years before a real bond was established. During that time, Peter and my son also became close in a gradual way. Sex was part of our courtship and we enjoyed it—but it too was not frantic or rushed. We were growing together on so many levels; sex was just one combination among many. And never the most important."

PETER'S STORY: Peter, forty-seven, is a big, bearded man—quiet, warm, and attractive. He was raised in New York, an only child, by his maternal grandparents after his parents were divorced. His mother spent most of his growing-up years on the stage and although there were a lot of visits, he couldn't really depend on her for his daily routines. He describes himself in those days as a child who became quite self-sufficient on the surface—"a tough loner" who really yearned for more attention.

As a result, Peter's first experiences of dating in high school were "very intense." He was torn between fear of be-ing rejected and "wanting the experience of love so badly that I could barely stand it." He adds: "Sex was a definite thrill for me because it involved so much intimate contact and ful-fillment of my fantasy life, but it was also terrifying to some-one so needy. I was very easily won!" But like most high school boys, Peter was required to be "cool," to make it seem as if only the sex part mattered, when in fact he was most attracted to the emotional aspects of being with girls.

While at college in the East, Peter continued to be more or less a loner until he became involved with one woman in a relationship that lasted three years. They were comfortable together, sexually happy, and although Peter wasn't ready to be married, he felt relieved and thankful to have a close re-lationship. "She reassured me in a very basic way that I was a worthy partner and someone who deserved to be loved."

After they broke up (because Peter was unwilling to marry at the time), Peter returned to his former uninvolved status but felt good about it. Most of his time and energy were spent developing his business—an activity he thoroughly enjoyed. He had only one other relationship prior to Anne. "I had my share of one-nighters, but they weren't very rewarding. Sex for me really required a commitment to someone, and I was just too engrossed in myself and my work to be open to any-one. It was too distracting."

When Peter and Anne met, Peter was thirty-four and "pretty much the perennial bachelor." They were introduced by mutual friends, partly for business reasons. Peter describes his response to Anne: "We were united in some way almost from the moment we met. I sensed that Anne was a very unique, complete person. We didn't need each other but we wanted to spend more and more time together. We did this under the pretext of business. Working together provided a way for me to make a commitment to her."

Peter saw in Anne "a reason for me to have a life companion," and when he decided to marry her and become father to her son (and later their own second son), "it was the best decision I ever made."

Some Questions and Answers

Why did you stop having sex?

PETER: To be honest, and with all due respect to couples who will enjoy it forever, sex became fairly routine for us and not more rewarding than making love without sex. *Anne* never became boring to me but orgasms did. Not totally boring *during* sex, but I would feel often wiped out afterward and think, "This is not where I want to put my energies, and it does not make me feel closer to Anne."

ANNE: To me, sex feels like a way to get to know someone. It's what attracts you at first but once you know them, sex is no longer so necessary. At least this has been my experience. I had a lot of sex in my first marriage and kept trying to get close to my husband and never did. With Peter, we have very little actual sex and a huge amount of closeness and love. Maybe we just are people who don't need a lot of sex together.

Why did you become celibate two years ago—at that point in your marriage?

PETER: Well, we say that's when we started being celibate but actually our sexual activity has slowly waned over the years. It just seemed more honest to say we were celibate when we finally acknowledged it two years ago. By admitting our status to each other, we avoided falling into the trap of secretly thinking something was wrong with us. *We* knew it was okay for us to be together and in love and not have sex, but we didn't know anyone who we were sure would agree. So it was a private affirmation of the value of our marriage without sex.

ANNE: I think I always knew we'd be celibate one day. Sex was good but it never had kept up with our love. I actually looked forward to being celibate. When we knew we weren't going to have more children, sex became less significant somehow. I know that sounds positively Victorian, but that's how I felt. I am just as happy—I would say even more so—to be in Peter's arms or to hold him in mine.

Do you talk to your children about your being celibate and do you think that it has a different effect on them from when you were more sexual together?

ANNE: We never discussed our private sexual lives with them and we don't discuss our private celibate lives. What they know about sex is that it's something reserved for love, but that you certainly don't have to have sex to show someone you love them. They see us behave (usually) in quite loving ways toward each other, and I think they have a good feeling about their parents' marriage. And naturally, they know every detail of the sexual culture that they want to—we certainly don't refuse them information about sex. We just let them know it's not *our* number-one priority as adults.

How do you each integrate being celibate with your experience of being a man or a woman?

PETER: When I was younger, sex was on my mind a lot, but as I grow older, it seems to mean less and less to me. I know it is almost an obsession for American men. And maybe all men. Men together talk about sex constantly, especially in my business. Really, almost all the jokes in construction are sexual. And I'll talk like that on the job, too—it's the language you learn. But when I'm with Anne, and since we've been celibate, sex is much less of an issue to me. I think that being celibate has made me feel more integrated as a man. I experience myself as a multidimensional man—one with feelings, ideas, a creative mind, a humorous soul, etc. There is something strong to me about being celibate—being self-contained, powerful, virile. And yet still loving, warm, and tender.

ANNE: I see being celibate right now as being myself. In my early years, I never knew why people wanted to keep being virgins. I thought it was ridiculous, false, and prudish—that a real woman was a sexual woman. Now I have a much better appreciation for why a woman (or a man) might want to preserve her sexuality for a time when she knows that it represents how she really feels.

I have never really thought it was right to be defined as a woman by my sexuality. I am this person who happens to be a woman, and sex is somewhere on the list of things I can do, along with painting, dancing, cooking, etc. I do them all pretty well and none of them regularly.

Being celibate for me means being celibate *with* Peter. I don't know if I could have this with another man because our being celibate is based on the strength of our marriage.

Michael and Ginny

Michael and Ginny are in their fourth year of marriage and have been celibate for more than two years. They are a dynamic, vivacious couple who obviously enjoy each other deeply and are not afraid of showing their feelings. One does not have the impression at all of repressed sexuality smoldering under the surface, about to erupt. They seem altogether comfortable and happy.

GINNY'S STORY: Ginny is a very pretty thirty-five-year-old woman with a fluid, carefree personality. She grew up in a wealthy Southern family who moved to a New York suburb when Ginny was nine. She was the oldest of three children. Her family was always very loving and very open with each other. Ginny began having sex at the age of fifteen. In the sophisticated high school she attended, this was typical behavior and "sex was what you did on a date." When she was sixteen, her father, an executive with the telephone company, was transferred to a Midwest city and Ginny was easily the most "hip" girl in her new high school class.

Ginny entered a "Big 10" university and joined a sorority; within two months "I became a freak." The drug era provided her with a lifestyle "which I absolutely loved." For the next three years, Ginny was the "most far-out" woman on the campus. "I went easily from politics into uninhibited hedonism." Still, she managed to graduate. Although she "definitely lived for the next party," Ginny had a serious side that kept her focused on her schoolwork.

As a "joyous hippie," Ginny enjoyed the freedom of "moment-to-moment" sex and the spontaneity of sleeping with everyone she wanted. When she met Michael, she was immediately taken with the strength of his personality and his radiance, "so unlike most of the men I had been with." He made it clear to her that he wasn't interested in a sexual thing, but that he was attracted to her in a profound way and wanted to pursue a friendship. His commitment to a "life of higher goals" had a deep appeal to her.

MICHAEL'S STORY: Michael is thirty-nine years old, an industrial engineer with a major national corporation. He is a very handsome man with movie-star good looks who glows with youth and health. Michael grew up in an upper-middle-class home in the suburbs of Detroit where he and Ginny now live. He has two older brothers and has always been close to his family.

Michael describes himself as a "long-time seeker." He had always had the thought of being a priest, but since his family wasn't Catholic, "it didn't seem like a very practical choice." He attended a Midwestern university where he discovered first radical politics, then drugs. He dropped out of the university twice and ended up moving to San Francisco. He pursued an interest in film, becoming a film distributor for a time, but then left for Europe. "I didn't find what I wanted there," so he returned again to the Bay Area, where he decided to become a farmer. He learned to farm and garden skillfully enough to become the caretaker on several large estates and loved the work. During this time he became interested in Eastern meditation as well. He eventually made his way back to the Midwest, where he completed his education and where he has continued to explore and develop his inner life, as well as becoming a very successful engineer.

Michael reports that he was not very sexually active in high school and tended to back away from sexual experiences that were available to him. He thinks that he "thought about sex far less" than the other boys in his class. He "didn't know much about girls," coming from an all-male family and felt he had a lot to learn about them in all areas, not just the sexual. He had one steady girlfriend, and he was happy with the nonsexual relationship.

In the spring of his freshman year at the university, he slept with a woman for the first time and enjoyed the experience. In the next year, he slept with about thirty more women and "although it was fun, I didn't like how I felt afterwards—sort of physically run-down and drained."

In San Francisco, he maintained a fairly active sex life, but his interest was not that strong. As he grew away from drugs and started turning to the life of a farmer, he began to explore Eastern mysticism, meditation, and spirituality. He read Yogananda's *Autobiography of a Yogi* and "although I didn't have any intellectual understanding of celibacy, I had a gut-level feeling that celibacy would be a great aid in spiritual development."

When Michael met Ginny back in his home town, he had been celibate for a year and was quite committed to the experience. But he fell deeply in love with Ginny and had a strong intuition that "I was going to take care of this woman." Their love grew to a point where a commitment was called for, and Michael became "uneasy," wondering if his spiritual goals would be compatible with marriage. He remembers a friend saying "There's so little love in the world; don't restrict yours." He eventually became more comfortable in the relationship and felt more ready.

They had a long engagement of eight months, during which they were physical but not sexual together. "It was like courting." The tender, devotional aspect of their love grew, and they were married.

After they were married, Ginny and Michael made love sexually but felt that "sex wasn't as significant as it had been in our previous relationships with others." By about the third month, they were sexual only about once a week, feeling that "other aspects of our lives were more exciting to us." After about a year and a half, they decided to be celibate altogether and have been so for the past two and a half years.

Some Questions and Answers

Were you sexually attracted to each other when you met?

MICHAEL: Yes. Very much so, but the sexuality was more diffused than localized in its feeling—it felt more cosmic and universal than just specific and genital.

When you became less sexual after three months of marriage, did you think it was "normal?"

GINNY: Well, we thought it was normal because we talked about it, and it was what we wanted. Actually, I thought intellectually that we maybe *should* be having more sex, but it wasn't because I felt the desire for more sex, it just seemed more socially "correct" to be more sexual, but we would laugh about it.

MICHAEL: I had the feeling that sexual activity was not a necessity—I had heard of celibate marriages. After a time, the physiological need wasn't there, and it seemed more abnormal to have sex than not to.

Did you feel uncomfortable with your sexual desires once you decided to be celibate?

MICHAEL: Actually, it was the other way around. The desire seemed to decrease, and then I thought about celibacy. It was a great relief, as well as a great kind of freedom, to be free of sexual desire—it felt so comfortable.

Are you still at all physically attracted to each other?

GINNY: I've actually grown more physically attracted to Michael over the past three years, but I've learned to direct that physical energy in other ways. The desire automatically dissolves into waves of lovingness and the expansion of my heart toward him.

MICHAEL: I like the pleasure I derive from Ginny's "foxiness." She is a very physically beautiful woman, and I definitely prefer her to other women in a physical way. Our romance, like other romances, certainly has sexual attraction as one aspect. But the sexuality is just allowed to float into deeper feelings of love. We get much happier in this way than when we were sexual.

Do you have any kind of physical relationship?

MICHAEL: Absolutely. We sleep together and hug and kiss and touch, but we don't pursue sex. Really, we have no physical boundaries at all. We feel deeply physically connected all the time and sex would more likely disrupt that flow than enhance it.

GINNY: What it has been like is a very long, delicate courtship and *very romantic*. It's ideal for a woman, you know—to have that tender side of a man always turned toward you.

Do your families know you are celibate?

GINNY: Definitely not. We would never discuss it with our parents. It's not a *cause* for us. At this point, although it is very natural for us, it's very private. Also, our parents want us to have children, and right now we're not sure we want to. But children and celibacy are two very different issues for us, and we don't want our families to confuse the two. Some of our close friends know and seem very intrigued by the idea of celibacy. We know two other couples who are celibate as well.

Do you recommend celibacy to couples?

MICHAEL: Obviously, we think it is a good idea for us because it has created such a smooth, loving relationship for us, and like we said, it feels very natural for us. But if it isn't natural, it would probably be a premature decision on the part of a couple. One thing to realize is that celibacy seems to arrive in marriage as something valuable. If a couple becomes less sexual together, it may be because their relationship requires more delicate kinds of love experiences than sexual activity. Then being celibate is a great way to explore that love. It seems to us like a step in evolution of love—from sex to celibacy.

Celibacy and the Growth of Consciousness

The history of human sexuality is the evolution of consciousness.

——HERBERT RICHARDSON

7 It is well known that one's body, thoughts, and emotions all function together—interdependently. This is the fundamental outlook of Eastern health and medicine. But in the West there has always been the tendency until recently to separate these functions. We go to one group of doctors for treatment of the body and another for treatment of the mind and emotions. With the advent of the holistic health movement, this piecemeal approach to human functioning is changing back to the treatment of the whole person, in keeping with the physiologists' view of integrated mind-body development. The study of human physiology is really the study of how the mind, emotions, and body all mutually support each other. This is also the study of human consciousness. How aware one is at any given moment—how alert, perceptive, intelligent, loving—that is, how "conscious"—is based on the entire functioning of one's physiology at the time.

Under most circumstances, whether we know it or not,

175

growing increasingly more conscious is the better part of human development. In fact, the growth of consciousness is considered by many to be *the* essential purpose of life. Its ultimate goal is to bring about a state of permanent fulfillment in the individual.

Scientist-philosopher Julian Huxley had this to say about the growth toward fulfillment: "Fulfillment seems to describe better than any other single word the positive side of human development and human evolution—the realization of inherent capacities by the individual and of new possibilities by the race; the satisfaction of needs, spiritual as well as material; the emergence of new qualities of experience to be enjoyed."[1]

In order to experience fulfillment, Huxley goes on to say, we need to develop lives in harmony with our "basic inner necessities" as much as in harmony with others, based on the evolutionary need to be as great as we can be, because, says Huxley, "No man ever achieves his real self until he is his best self."

In their original intent and most significant aspects, the rituals and structures of religion are designed to elicit the response of the growth of consciousness. This is the essential lesson in Judaism's Kabbalah, in Christ's teachings, in the mystic doctrines of medieval alchemy, in the Eastern religions—in short, in practically all spiritual quests, past and present.

The growth of consciousness is also the primary message of modern psychology. As we look for ways to express love and creativity and ways to enhance mental and emotional experiences, what we are really seeking are ways to develop or unfold consciousness. It is this inner development of consciousness that leads to progressively more satisfying life experiences.

EVOLVING TO CELIBACY

Becoming celibate seems to occur spontaneously—like other natural events—in keeping with particular social, emotional,

and spiritual needs and desires and with a corresponding minimizing of sexual urgency. This description of the celibate experience is at the heart of almost every discussion one has
with people practicing celibacy.

If the possibility of celibacy is natural for some people at
certain times, then there must be some aspect of human development which can enable this experience to come about
naturally.

Celibacy outside religious life is very new to our society.
Yet it seems to be emerging *now*, in an age of increasing emphasis on self-development, expansion of inner boundaries,
wholeness of life, strengthening the society from within. The
focus is more and more on new ways of relating to each other,
new modes of interpersonal expression that take people beyond the ordinary experiences of daily routine. As personal
goals change in line with the evolution of inner lives, sexuality is changing as well. Dr. June Singer has written: "Evolutionary consciousness heralds the new age. . . . We are aware
of how much we can control our sexuality and of the ramifi-
cations of all the ways in which we do control it." And, she
continues: "The new era we are entering will require a shift
from the exclusively personal viewpoint to one that includes
the transpersonal, a shift from an egocentric position toward
a universal orientation. . . . The new model of sexual consciousness will need to be inward-turning for . . . in order to be aware
of oneself as a cosmic being, one needs to discover the nature
of his own essence. . . ."[2]

One direction of that inward model is the turn toward becoming celibate. There is no doubt that such a shift is in keeping with the growth of consciousness. As Herbert Richardson
has proposed, "Even to imagine the possibility that sexual desire can be renounced involves the presence of a new kind of
consciousness."

In light of this new awareness, it is only natural that all
aspects of sexuality be evaluated—not just *how* you are having sex or with whom but whether you really want to or not,
whether having sex is in keeping at any given time with all
other developments going on in your life.

There are those who believe that having sex is opposed to the growth of consciousness, at least sex with orgasm. Because when you have an orgasm, you actually lose consciousness for a moment. The other times loss of consciousness occurs are during sleep, during illness (i.e., when you faint or are in a coma), or when you are overly intoxicated from some drug such as alcohol. Now, it is true that loss of consciousness during sex usually occurs for only seconds at most. But according to neurologist Richard Mayeux, reporting in the *New England Journal of Medicine*, it has been found that some people "experience a profound amnesia and disorientation for several hours after having sexual intercourse."

In the eleventh and twelfth centuries, notes Richardson, sex was considered sinful for just this reason: "Because it involved the temporary suspension of man's reason and voluntary freedom...at least in the moment of orgasm."

Sex therapists today often advise their clients to allow themselves to *lose* consciousness during sex in order to have a "full" experience of it, in order to get them to stop thinking and analyzing during sex. As William Masters writes, "To a degree your own pleasure is dulled because you are not lost in the experience—you're observing. I am *not* saying that you experience no pleasure at all. I'm just saying that some of it is blocked. A level of perception is blocked."

So losing consciousness during lovemaking or being "lost" in the experience is said to be beneficially pleasurable. But for those who are fully "there," who can maintain full alertness, observing is a very natural part of all experience—not something to avoid but something that increases enjoyment. And actually, one is really only fully appreciative of something if one is *not* lost in it. By remaining within oneself, centered, aware, not overwhelmed by the experience, the chances are that the experience will be much more full, more clearly perceived, felt, understood, and enjoyed. This happens because as humans we have the unique capability of experiencing something and simultaneously being aware that we are experiencing it. So when we're having a good time, we *know* we're having a good time. But if we are doing something that *ought* to be pleasurable (from past experience) and isn't, we're aware that we're *not* having a good time. And indeed such a situation occurs when there has been a change in consciousness and explains why desires, including sexual ones, change throughout one's life.

So the next question is, What is there in the development of consciousness that could lead a person to give up voluntarily that which affords so many of us such great pleasure?

THE NATURE OF PLEASURE

We can start by looking at the changing field of sexuality and consciousness from the view of physiology and ask, Isn't sex always instinctively desirable in that it is always physically pleasurable? The answer is yes and no. We are biologically structured to experience sex as pleasure, but we are also biologically structured to become celibate—to experience the growth from one kind of pleasure to other, perhaps more "pleasurable" pleasures.

According to Masters and Johnson, the basic physiological sexual responses remain the same regardless of the kind of activity used to achieve them. So we can conclude that although it's natural to be sexually responsive, the response itself doesn't really grow as one matures. And if other pleasures begin to replace the sexual response, the response can in fact diminish and give way to other kinds of more complex human pleasures such as emotions and ideas. As one kind of pleasure is replaced by a higher form of pleasure, the lower form is thus inhibited. As an example, women may experience feelings of contentment and deep joy during pregnancy and these feelings often serve as inhibitors of sexual desire.

Behavioral researcher H. J. Campbell presents a good summary of this transformation of physiology. He defines pleasure as "simply the name we give to the subjective feeling we experience when our limbic areas are electrically active."

He concludes that "the pursuit of pleasure is the *only* form of behavior" because when the pleasure areas are active, the impulses they generate reduce the electrical activity of the other behavioral areas.

The pleasure-seeking behavior of humans has a sexual component based on the male sex hormone found in both male and female that maintains the degree of pleasure seeking. But at the same time, sexual functioning is the *sole* physiological process individuals do sacrifice for any number of reasons—whether for a higher goal or simply as a matter of convenience. "Everyone rejects sexual stimuli," observed Masters and Johnson, "when he feels that the circumstances are inappropriate." Or as Silvano and James Arieti contend, "Sexual pleasure may be the precursor of another type of pleasure that consists of spiritual and intangible qualities." This view of sexual development is based on the changes that can and do occur in one's physiological growth.

Campbell found that most long-term sexual relations were not rewarding if the partners continued to seek only autonomic sensory input during sex. Sexual sensory pleasure, he observed, is not generally progressive: it does not keep up with the growth one experiences in other areas. What Campbell suggests is that for sex to continue to be pleasurable, in keeping with other developments, people learn to derive sexual pleasure "not from sexual sensory input but from the descending impulses from higher regions." In other words, sex grows to be a mental pleasure more than a sensory pleasure and becomes infused in higher-level experiences. To explain this growth, Campbell outlines three stages of pleasure seeking in humans:

1. Feeling-doing—an early stage where there is mostly sensory input and little higher level activity, such as thinking or intellect usage.

2. Thinking-doing—a stage where thought is turned into action which impacts on the environment and which includes most of life's activities. At the highest level of this stage would be creative expressions of thought, such as music and art.

3. Just *thinking* as a source of pleasure. This highest stage of human pleasure is found in mathematical and philosophical thought—where thought itself, without expressed activity, provides pleasure.

Campbell's physiological approach to the way we as humans learn and are physically prepared to experience pleasure is based on progressive and evolutionary growth from pure sensory experience to pure thought experience.

> Gradually, as brain maturation proceeds, the importance of sensory input declines. It never becomes irrelevant, but eventually the higher regions are sufficiently developed anatomically and informationally so that interchange between the thinking regions and the pleasure areas can be largely self-sustaining.[3]

Even animals have been found to want to progress beyond pure sensory reward. For example, rats that have been trained to use both a simple maze and a longer, more complicated one, when given a choice of a route to obtain food choose the more complicated maze.

But so far as we know, only humans derive pleasure from thought *itself*. And as Campbell maintains, "The clearest distinction we can make between the subhuman and human is that the human is able to evoke electrical activity in the limbic pleasure areas by processes occurring in the thinking region of the brain."

A scientist at work in the laboratory may not be regarded as someone having fun, but that's often exactly what's going on. Pleasure in one's work where one's mind is constantly stimulated and enlivened is an exclusively human source of pleasure and one that does not require any sensory input.

Albert Einstein is one famous example of a person who experienced much of his joy of discovery purely on the mental level, without any experience of the sensory world he was dealing with. In fact, his most profound theoretical or "mental" discoveries were not even verified in the physical world until many years later.

Higher emotional responses such as unconditional love are another nonsensory source of pleasure. And in fact, "the human brain can reach such a degree of sophistication" that one will lay down one's life for someone else or even for an idea. This kind of pleasure is exemplified in Wolman's Antigone Principle—a psychological model of altruism. Antigone is remembered for her willingness to die to uphold the dignity of her deceased brother, believing her sacrifice to be the most just and, to her, the most meaningful act possible. This principle is reiterated in the many human experiences where love draws a response greater than life itself: "This is my commandment: love one another, as I have loved you. A man can have no greater love than to lay down his life for friends" (John 15:12–13).

In light of the above, one can see that a person may *easily* give up the lower pleasures for the higher pleasures if his or her "pleasure response" is thus developed. What may seem like a great sacrifice from a lower-pleasure standpoint may feel very natural and right from a higher-pleasure standpoint.

This is one psychophysiological explanation for how we as humans advance. As sensory pleasure becomes more refined, higher states of consciousness are experienced. So as higher human pleasures come to replace lower ones, intellectual and emotional functions may minimize or inhibit sexual response.

Remembering that as one develops, sex becomes more complex and more mental, it is not surprising that this growth of consciousness could lead to another option—one of no sex, or celibacy—if sex is replaced by other mental, emotional, or spiritual pleasures. Although in Western culture it is much less clear how celibacy fits into and advances psychosexual growth than in the East, this idea is nonetheless found in many of the developmental theories of Western psychology—where sexuality is understood as "one step along the way to developing the capacity to love."

The eminent philosopher Pierre Teilhard de Chardin describes the growth of human life as a series of steps in which a person integrates his self-love, his social life, and his orientation to God or spiritual life. Teilhard labels these steps of growth: affectionization, sensitization, and universalization. You begin the process by becoming "self-centered"—by becoming aware of yourself, and yourself in the context of sexual desires. Once comfortable with your own sexuality, you can become "socialized." According to Teilhard, it is only those of us who have really confronted the depths of our own sexuality, not only socially but physically as well, who feel comfortable as sexual beings, who are able to be fully socialized. And there are those who continue to grow beyond socialization to a "universalized" experience of sexuality—where tenderness and compassion are felt for all aspects of natural life. Thus, for some universalized people, celibacy is a kind of culmination of sexual maturity and development, enabling one to have the experience of universal love.

Teilhard's outlook is very similar to Abraham Maslow's. According to Maslow's research, the highest human need is "self-actualization" or the need to fulfill one's human potential. The higher needs are the more integrated, the more human responses which incorporate more of a person's capacities. In Maslow's hierarchy of needs, self-actualization comes after physiological and safety needs and after the needs for affection, achievement, and esteem. When we choose, Maslow says, we choose the higher need over the lower one, if we've been experiencing both.

In this "needs" progression, Maslow found that genital abstinence or celibacy is not in any way psychologically harmful in the most integrated, most self-actualized people functioning at the highest levels of human expression. What he found was that one's intellectual and emotional understanding and attitude toward celibacy is what makes it healthy or not. He found that self-actualized people preferred abstinence to the kind of sex without emotional or psychological commitment. (He also found that when they *are* sexual, they tend to enjoy it more intensely than others.)

If we compare Maslow's version of psychosexual development with Freud's, there is an interesting similarity. In both views, growth from one level of pleasure to the next is required for full development. However, instead of one growing in a sense "freer" of sexual dominance, as in Maslow's needs progression, Freud held that as one progressed, one's sexuality became more inhibited and sublimated. Maslow's view is of love-based sexuality; Freud's view is sex-based love, with all energy as sublimated sexual energy expressed in various psychic ways. For Freud, sexuality was the prime mover of the human psyche and the only source of human energy. He proposed that all love and creativity—all the higher pleasures—are "aim-inhibited sexuality."

Many others such as Erich Fromm, Alfred Adler, and Carl Jung disputed this theory. They saw that if one carried Freud's analysis—that all human emotion and activity is sublimated sexuality—to its logical extreme, if sex were never inhibited there would be no tender love. They realized that there must be a *nonsexual* source for tenderness and love. For them, it was love, not sex, that formed the basis for their views of human behavior. Freud placed a heavy emphasis on sexual energy as the origin of behavior and was able to adapt his theory to all manifestations of human nature. But sometimes he had to bend a little to accommodate his observations. Such was the case with celibacy.

In Freudian terms, celibacy would be total sublimation of sexuality—a desexualization of drives into a generalized love for everyone. Because Freud theorized that sex was the primary motivating force of human life, one would suspect, as June Singer has, that the Freudian view would leave "hardly any place for a legitimate celibacy."

However, Freud was surprisingly open to the positive results of celibacy. He observed that people can achieve happiness by transcending sexuality for a higher experience of love and took examples from the religious life. He cites St. Francis of Assisi as the celibate who "went furthest in thus exploiting love for the benefit of an inner feeling of happiness." He wrote:

> These people make themselves independent of their object's acquiescence by transferring the main value from the fact of being loved to their own act of loving; they protect themselves against loss of it by attaching their love not to individual objects but all men equally, and they avoid the uncertainties and disappointments of genital love by turning away from its sexual aim and modifying the instinct into an impulse with an inhibited aim.[4]

In an article entitled "A Psychoanalyst's Case for Celibacy," Dr. Jean Rosenbaum echoes this aspect of Freud's evaluation in observing that celibacy, far from creating neuroses through the sublimation of sexuality, can serve to make manifest a great love and affection for all humankind and the "desexualization of drives can be thus turned into 'works of service,' benefiting society as greatly as 'any creative life work.'" Perhaps then, in Freudian ideology, the celibate is able to reexperience the pregenital sexuality that Freud speaks of as "oceanic"—where love and sex are not divided but begin together.

The Freudian view that all human expression and the development of culture is really a sublimation of sexual energy was an interesting assessment of the mechanics of the development of consciousness. But Freud's concern with this transformation was to establish the true value of sexuality in all experience. The idea of a changing sexual energy was valid, but Freud no doubt overestimated the primacy of sexuality by placing it in the center of human development, instead of recognizing that, transformed, it became another form of energy.

Other Western psychologists—Jung in particular—broadened this understanding to include all psychic energy. Jung showed how human psychic energy could flow in a number of channels, including love, intellect, and creative and religious experiences. For him, the primary life force includes the sexual but is not based on it.

SEXUAL ENERGY: GAIN OR DRAIN?

Conduct the water which is flowing into the sewer to the garden instead.

————ST. AUGUSTINE

Throughout history, a universal idea has prevailed that sexual energy for nonprocreative purposes can either be "used up" in sexual activity or "contained" for upholding the development of the body and the mind. This sex energy was seen as the fuel for opening these channels of experience, not only in the East but in the alchemy of the Europeans during the sixteenth and seventeenth centuries. Moses was said to have requested soldier-husbands to refrain from marital sex to preserve their strength for battle. Ralph Waldo Emerson, when married, was also a believer in sexual abstinence for preserving his energy and wrote "I husband all my strength in this bachelor life I lead."

Even today there are people everywhere who maintain that physical orgasm has a draining effect on both mind and body that results in an overall energy loss in the system. To prevent this loss, many athletes, actors, musicians, and other performers forego sex before the game, the show, the concert. Basketball player Bill Walton once estimated that about half the players he knew found it helpful to abstain before a game. The idea is that sexual energy is thus converted into a better performance.

Taken at its most superficial value, such a view may appear repressive and "prerevolutionary." But if one explores it in more depth, this understanding of human sexual energy finds a surprising amount of support from a number of diverse sources.

In his scholarly work on Eastern philosophy, Mircea Eliade wrote: "Modern science agrees with the ancient sages of the East... that what holds the universe together is the mysterious, non-individualized something we call 'energy.'"

R. Buckminster Fuller, the great synergistic thinker, helps us conceive of energy as a concept of wholes, not as discrete entities or parts. According to Fuller and others, an energy *system* or "whole" is the only valid way that energy has any functional meaning. Science presents this theory with the understanding that matter and energy are inseparable... and that the universe holds together based on their natural interconnectedness.

When this understanding of wholeness is applied to human sexuality, sexual energy is seen as a part of a larger, more universal energy. Sexuality becomes, as Jung and others saw, "only one way of expressing bodily and spiritually, that universal energy" that is incarnated in every human being, a universal energy that expresses itself through all of nature, which humans can express within their own lives however they choose. This is essentially the Eastern concept of the relationship between sexual and universal energy.

In the East, the expansion of consciousness and the transformation of sexual energy have been generally observed to be highly correlated events. Whether it is the expansion of consciousness that precedes any change in sexuality or the physiological results of the refinement of sexuality that bring about the expansion of consciousness is not really clarified since both events are considered virtually inseparable.

In this view, sexual energy has two purposes: one is procreation and the other is its usefulness in the transformation of consciousness—from a near-animal state to a universal consciousness of God; from "unconscious" to "all-conscious."

In order to accomplish this growth more quickly, the East has long promoted the use of traditional methods for raising the level of consciousness through techniques that serve to redirect energy within the body. Meditation and yoga practices help refine mental and physical energy, enabling the mind and body to function in a more efficient, coherent way. It is said that as physical energy is refined inwardly, it creates a more powerful base of functioning for all outward activities.

This transformation brings about some changes in physiology and some consequent changes in consciousness. To maintain this evolutionary process of accelerating the growth of consciousness, there are those who practice celibacy along with other technologies, believing it to aid in the transformation of energy. They contend that if one doesn't discharge sexual energy in orgasm, it becomes converted into other levels of energy. The idea is that the cells are revitalized by a high frequency of energy generated throughout the body, keeping one vibrant by maintaining a vitality of body and mind.

As a form of self-actualization of the body that is integrated with mental powers, whether achieved with the help of celibacy or not, this higher integration of mind-body functioning enables one to establish spirituality as a physical reality. The "magic" powers attained by various people throughout history were also said to be related to the physical manifestation of this high psychic energy.

Sexual desire is thus understood as one step in a series of energy transformations which bring about the growth of consciousness. In a person who is entirely "unconscious," says Elisabeth Haich, "the possibility of a transformation of energy does not even occur.... Therefore, he simply expends physical-sexual powers in a normal way, and not creative-spiritual ones." And if one tries to be celibate but is not physiologically ready for the experience, this is a form of repression of sexuality. The natural development only occurs because consciousness is based on a physiological readiness.

This formulation has been put forth to explain the mutual

refinement of human consciousness and sexuality as well as certain aspects of human evolution. From this perspective, there are stages through which mankind evolves from an unconscious state to a dawning of consciousness, to an emotional life perhaps involving a spouse and family, to a desire for knowledge, to an inner awakening of creative expression, to a realization of universal and divine love and, finally, to a universal awareness manifested in a universal unity of consciousness.

Initially, society itself helps refine sexuality from its most self-serving to its most loving nature, the process John Gagnon and William Simon refer to as socialization of sexuality. In many cultures young people have been taught to postpone sexual fulfillment for some time. During this waiting time, sexual tension increases and when it does not get released, it gets transformed into a more complex social awareness which has been awakened by the desire.

The sexual urge thus gives way to a "higher," more lasting level of fulfillment—that of being in love. Richardson explains: "In persons who have attained a certain level of psychosexual integration, genital feeling is aroused only in conjunction with particular beloved persons, and the primary satisfaction gained from sexual intercourse is not orgasm but communion." From this channeling of energy into love comes a further development in the evolution of consciousness—the desire for creative expression.

Most experts seem to agree, no matter what the mechanics they favor, that sexual energy is somehow associated with creativity. But whether celibacy is a requirement for its favorable expression or not has been debated for centuries. According to one historian, in ancient times, the Muses were represented as virgins "to show the little disposition which the learned have for physical love."

Honoré de Balzac put it bluntly: "If you sleep with a woman, you leave your novel in her bed." As for Tolstoi: "Oh, if only I could be free from desire for three hours—how much more I could create." For Thoreau, writing in *Walden*, chastity represented all that was best in man's creative development: "Chastity is the flowering of man; and what are called Genius, Heroism, Holiness and the like are but various fruits which succeed it."

In the beginning of this century, Dr. Arthur Gould even proposed that "all our great thinkers have affirmed the physical, mental and spiritual benefits to be derived from absolute chastity." We may not agree but even today, Dr. Mary Calderone, a leading authority on sexuality, defines creativity as "simply the result of the evolution of the person to the point at which fulfillment of his highest potential becomes as easy for him as breathing." She goes on to explain how creative experiences may or may not require sexual tension at their base. But she reasons that as one grows in maturity and self-development, eroticism may well *decrease* and creativity increase: "As the individual matures (in the true as well as chronological sense), as his experiences of self and others deepen...his eroticism might appear to diminish, whether absolutely or relatively; but if the individual is free, the total in terms of creativity, should, I believe, increase."[5]

For a long time, Freud's theory identifying creativity as sublimated sexuality made creativity seem like a kind of second-class sexuality—valid, but not The Real Thing. But with the broader picture coming from Eastern sources as well as from Jung, Maslow, and others, it is clear that the transformation of sexual energy into creative experience is a spontaneous consequence of human evolution and the development of consciousness and not a negative repression of an equally natural function—sex. Neither creativity nor sexuality is more "real"—both represent human nature in different states of consciousness. And these aspects of development can only be meaningfully experienced if they occur naturally.

As Consciousness Rises

The refinement of consciousness and the refinement of sexual energy must be natural to be valid. Psychologists and others are careful to warn against trying to finesse stages of growth. They indicate that the physiological, psychological, and spiritual development of the individual has to be coherent and integrated. Consciousness demands balance in growth. That is why *no one becomes celibate independent of other aspects of change in consciousness.* Clearly, it's good to be as fully acquainted with sex as necessary, particularly if one harbors constant worries that something is being missed that would bring pleasure. If it is a sacrifice to give it up, why give it up? No self-respecting seeker renounces something for the sake of something less, only for the sake of something more.

However, there are some individuals for whom sex holds no fascination, presumably because they are experiencing levels of pleasure higher than the sexual. This comes about because apparently, as consciousness rises, one doesn't miss sex. There is a calmness, a clarity of understanding, certainly not a hysterical rejection. And as consciousness develops, giving up sexual activity is easy because other experiences are providing more enjoyment than sex. If there were no better pleasures, there would be no reason to give up sex. Obviously, the great saints of the West and the great masters of the East would never have willingly renounced sexual pleasures if such pleasure could have brought them *lasting* fulfillment.

And it is at these higher levels of consciousness that the *desire* for sexual activity is said to "fall away like ripe fruit from a tree." Of course, sexual activity is still always available to such a person but is rarely chosen as a rewarding pleasure. So a natural desire for celibacy is said to occur. And the conserved energy is put to work in other ways, contributing, it is thought, to a strong and vital physiology that supports and maintains the permanent experience of higher levels of consciousness. Consequently, those who have achieved a permanent state of pleasure or fulfillment are said to radiate a kind of energy of love which is constant, unbounded, brilliant, and truly universal.

Attitudes for Celibacy

Letting Go of Sex

CELIBACY IN TODAY'S SOCIETY

8 Ours is a very different time from when Thomas Mann wrote, "The future is for the nations who are chaste" and from when Mary Baker Eddy observed that "chastity is the cement of civilization and progress." But there is the possibility in our present-day society that we are in an optimal position to benefit from celibacy— to enjoy the measure of its freedom without the harm of sexual repression. And, in fact, we may need to try it.

As a society, over the past twenty years, we've certainly promoted the idea that it's OK to be sexual. With the desire to overcome an unnaturally repressive past as a nation, we proceeded to push sexual expression to its limits with some highly unfortunate consequences. But our reactions to these consequences indicate that we're still not comfortable with our sexuality. Indeed, so unresolved about sex are we that the eminent French AIDS researcher Jacques Leibowitch, M.D., was led to observe: "How very American...to look at a disease as homosexual or heterosexual, as if viruses had the intelligence to choose between different inclinations of human behavior. ...Americans are simply obsessed by sex."[1]

If total sexual freedom had been a truly useful event in this society, leading to positive changes and at least the par-

tial elimination of antisocial behavior associated with unfulfilled sexual needs, the issue of celibacy would probably never
have come up. But actually, in the aftermath of the sexual liberation movement, when all that pent-up sexual tension
would surely have been released, the results were just the opposite. In the "liberated" early 1970s, mental illness struck one
out of four families, a murder was committed every seventy-
two minutes, fifteen violent crimes were committed every
hour. Without having to calculate exactly how much of this
societal misfortune was due to sexual causes, we may speculate that perhaps too much attention to sex was as debilitating to a society as too little.

Even before the arrival of AIDS, it was obvious that the
sexual revolution had not resolved our deepest fears, those
related to loving behavior, touching the places where we need
to grow in order to be very intimate with and very present
for our families, friends, and lovers, not to mention the larger
community.

For while we've been concentrating on being sexual, we've
neglected a lot of other paths of exchange. As Eugene Bianchi
observed, "On the level of mind and decision in the public
sphere, there is little or no intercourse between men and
women. In this realm, our . . . society is as celibate as a Trappist
monastery."

THE CELIBATE BALANCE

It is likely that if we were living in a way more "in tune" with
the laws of nature and evolution, there would be no need to
learn to be celibate because there would be no imbalance between sexual interest and human development, just as there
is no overindulgence among the animals or in the simpler human societies. And this imbalance is not just a present-day
phenomenon. As Bertrand Russell wrote in the earlier part of
this century:

> Sexual fatigue is a phenomenon introduced by civili-
> zation; it must be quite unknown among animals and

very rare among uncivilized men. In a monogamic marriage it is unlikely to occur except in a very small degree, since the stimulus of novelty is required with most men to lead them to physiological excess. It is also unlikely to occur when women are free to refuse their favours, for, in that case, like female animals, they will demand courtship before each act of intercourse, and will not yield their favours until they feel that a man's passions are sufficiently stimulated. This purely instinctive feeling and behaviour have been rendered rare by civilization.[2]

Celibacy may be one way to compensate for the overplay of sex. When sexual activity is overvalued and its "rest state" undervalued, the center of personal growth within the society may be off. Without knowledge of its unexpressed state, sexuality becomes diminished, unreplenished, and weakened. Celibacy allows sex to settle back into its full potential and, subsequently, provides the opportunity for society to reinvest in other channels of human communication that we seem to need badly.

Making Celibacy Conscious

> It makes no difference how we divert our attention
> from sexual desire, the main thing is that we divert it.
> ———ELISABETH HAICH

We overindulge primarily because we are constantly allowing ourselves to be aroused. So all techniques for celibacy pivot on giving the body a chance to rest, to get away from constant stimulation—to enable it to function in a different way.

There are really no instructions necessary for *becoming* celibate. All that is necessary is to *decide to be* celibate, for, as was pointed out in earlier chapters, celibacy is primarily a mental response. We can choose to be celibate, as we can choose to be sexual—*if* we are consciously able to choose at all. To be celibate as opposed to frustrated or martyred, one must make a conscious choice for a good reason—on behalf of one's own personal growth. And once we have chosen to be celibate for a time, the same principle applies to *remaining* celibate. To maintain celibacy, by far the best method, according to Haich and others is "never to lose hold of one's consciousness," to maintain clear awareness of what one wants.

The Celibate Vow

A conscious choice sometimes takes the form of a vow. In a vow, you give up something good for something you think will be even better. A vow of celibacy can be religious in nature. Traditionally, in religion, celibacy is pledged as a vow of faith. For example, in the West, the priests, nuns, and monks of the Catholic church renounce their sexual activity in favor of a commitment to Christ through a vow of chastity, along with other specific vows.

Or the vow to be celibate can be secular. One vows to be celibate to develop a fuller spiritual life or a more powerful love relationship. In the East, the *bramacharya* vow of celibacy is also more than a decision to avoid sex. It is a commitment to one's evolution based on the understanding that such a commitment is essential in order to experience higher states of consciousness and attain eventual permanent enlightenment. It is a dedication of the entire personality to a spiritual goal.

When we vow to love someone, either in marriage or another form of relationship, we envision that the situations in which we will love them "no matter what" will be smoothed over by the love we hold—that the growth of love through a commitment of devotion will be worth all the sacrifices along the way, that we will grow stronger and happier as we rise above all circumstances. Similarly, when one vows to be celibate in order to love more fully, there is the thought that the rewards of being celibate will exceed the sacrifice of sexual activity.

Thus, celibacy is not to be thought of as mere abstinence from sex, for that is what we all do most of the time anyway (at least most of us do). But it is more accurately understood as a conscious choice made on behalf of one's greater personal gain.

On the other hand, we certainly don't have to take a vow in order to be celibate. To maintain a celibate attitude does not require any vow at all. In fact, a vow could be decidedly wrong for some people, who would end up feeling bad if they broke it. So, for some, just keeping in mind that they're not going to have sex for a time is enough—just as for certain people, "not eating much" works a lot better than "going on a diet."

Whether or not it is an actual vow, once the mental decision to be celibate is made, it is the only real requirement for celibacy. It may have to be renewed from time to time, but it serves to set the activity of the body in a specific direction.

Mental Celibacy

The principle here is that thought decides activity. What we think determines what we do—what we have thought determines what we have done. So if you are going to be celibate, you have to instruct the mind to take a mental attitude of celibacy. And, in so doing, you would want to avoid the distraction of sexualized thought.

Masters and Johnson and others have recommended that when sex grows stale in a relationship, the couple pursue mental-fantasy exercises to generate more desire and interest in sex. We can assume that the opposite would hold true: in order to remain celibate (to be less sexually "desiring") you would *not* pursue active sexual fantasizing.

One method Elisabeth Haich recommends to gain mastery over sexuality is to "occupy the intellect with something else." She writes: "Two things cannot be in one and the same place at the same time. Therefore, we must expel all sexual thoughts from the intellect by replacing them with thoughts of a different kind.... We must learn to think about what it is we want to think about."[3]

This advice is not so simple to follow, however, especially if one doesn't have the kind of mind that can decide what it wants to think about. After all, if someone tells you not to think about elephants, what's the first thing you're thinking about? And if you're not *supposed* to think about sex, what else will the mind think about? So one must be relaxed about thinking; any sexual thought can come up, but you don't have to actively pursue it.

A modern priest, Joseph Wade, uses a simple approach. He counsels that, to maintain celibacy, one will do well to experience sexual feelings as "innocent, unreceived, and unwelcomed." He further advises to observe "a certain prudence" when dealing with the opposite sex, but he reminds us that a celibate individual "is not obliged to choose the more repressive and negative position in the manifestation of affection." In other words, you can be affectionate and loving even when celibate, as long as you don't encourage sexual desire. The key factor for a comfortable mental outlook on celibacy seems to be to keep it simple—and not to try and complicate the issue with behavioral analysis and rules. Celibacy is actually a lot less complicated than sexual activity—it involves doing nothing. So the best mental approach may be not to try at all—not to *try* to be sexual or *try* to be celibate. Just see what happens, keeping in mind what you want for yourself.

External Approaches to Physical Celibacy

To prevent specific arousal of localized sexuality in the body, sexually stimulating environments and physically arousing sensory experiences are naturally avoided. Sexual desire is said to be created through the senses. Impulses are sent from the brain, structuring the conditions for excitation. So celibacy is, of course, much easier to maintain when the senses are not bombarded by stimulants. Says Haich: "[There are] those people who do not leave their glands in peace, but rouse them with highly spiced food, stimulant drinks, erotic reading matter, films, and other such excitants. This only overtaxes the glands and weakens them prematurely."

In the East, advocates of celibacy have long recommended the avoidance of spicy foods such as garlic, onions, peppers, paprika, and the like. And, according to the *Kama Sutra*, eating the more alkaline foods will render continence easier.

In the West, Dr. William A. Alcott, a noted champion of

healthy living in the early nineteenth century, observed that sexual desire could be substantially decreased by the elimination of liquor, smoking, coffee, tea, condiments, sugar, lard, and spicy foods. "No man," he wrote, "has ever become an adulterer, a fornicator, an idolater eating simples such as plain wheat, corn, rye, potatoes, rice, peas, beans, turnips, apples." (One suspects that no man after eating such a diet was even able to move from the table!) Similarly, other sexual "energy savers" have outlined programs for celibate living that included going without tobacco and meat.

Foods generally regarded as aphrodisiacs would, of course, be avoided. Seafood has been most highly praised along these lines and would, therefore, be eaten with due respect. Snails are said to contain a sugar found in male seminal fluid and are thus thought to be highly "sexy."

Besides watching what one eats, advocates of celibacy have also advised increased participation in active sports, physical work, and specific exercises used to direct excess energy and the flow of blood into all parts of the body. In their book on hatha yoga, Michael Volin and Nancy Phelan recommended several yoga postures for maintaining celibacy. Among them are the eagle pose and the tree pose for males, the frog pose for females, and the shoulder stand for both, to help conduct the energy upward.

Volin and Phelan also note that in the East careful attention to the physical body is an important consideration in the maintenance of celibacy. Thorough bowel evacuation and bodily cleansing are said to help, along with some other activities for the more stoic, which include sleeping on a hard board, the requisite cold showers, and squatting over a basin of cool water while moving up and down slowly, immersing the genitals.* It is also said that sleeping on the back, which causes undue pressure from the bladder on the areas in question, should be avoided. Other recommendations include

---

*This, perhaps, could be modified by putting one's feet in cold water instead. Maimonides observed that when the feet become cold, sexual arousal is diminished.

tightening the buttocks for one to two minutes a day, pressing firmly on the perineum (for men).

A Word on Masturbation

A surprisingly large number of people wonder if masturbation is "permitted" if one is celibate. Since being celibate (whether for a day, a week, a year, or a lifetime) means refraining from sexual activity and since many books on sex have given masturbation the blue ribbon for most terrific orgasms, it is clear that if you want to indulge in celibacy, you don't masturbate.

It may seem that masturbation is a form of celibacy because you are generally alone when you do it, but since celibacy can be easily practiced by more than one person together, being alone is not a criterion for being celibate. Actually, masturbation is nothing if it is not sexual. It may be other things, too, but it is primarily a sexual activity, and since one wants to move away from being ruled by any behavior or any object of behavior, one may want to choose to avoid masturbation as one explores what it means to be celibate.

Notes from Tantric Technology: The Tao of Sex

The Tantrics were and still are considered the world experts in sexual knowledge and techniques for redirecting sexual energy. The Tantric approach is to experience one's sexuality not simply as an end state but also as a process through which the body is learning to evolve. The understanding that genital feeling can be transformed into a "higher sexual energy" carries with it the implication that sexuality is but one of the many ways the body can feel its own energy. Although the Tantrics were not strictly celibate, Tantric techniques for the transformation of sexual energy recognize the tremendous power of human sexuality and make use of it in ways that are often contrary to Western experience.

One basis for their techniques (which are essentially male-oriented) is the importance given to the value of semen for spiritual experience. Semen is considered to be the essential substance for male experience of higher consciousness and must therefore be conserved.

For the Tantric practitioner, the purpose of yoga practices is "to distill within the adept's body a golden liquid from which the elixir leading to longevity, immortality and mystical union could be formed." But being an adept is no simple matter. Volin and Phelan note that "as the celibate yogi conserves seminal energy through... transmutation, the Tantric also conserves it, even in the embrace of a woman, by hatha yoga techniques."

The most celebrated of the techniques used to redirect sexual energy is called *maithuna*. *Maithuna* is a ritualized procedure or extended technique for gaining control over one's sexuality generally during marriage. It is traditionally practiced during the first year of marriage. It involves the use of several techniques, ranging from meditation to the reabsorption of the discharged semen.* It is not only a physical technology but a symbolic one as well, in that the rite is understood to represent a symbolic union of divinity within the physical union of the married couple. The purpose of *maithuna* is to move beyond physical gratification to a state of permanent blissful fulfillment in marriage.

The ritual is described by Mircea Eliade, who writes: "In preparation, the two people retreat to some secluded place, such as a forest. Here the couple will spend many months in each other's company." For four months, the man is the woman's servant, continually available to her emotionally so his devotion to her may grow. First he sleeps in the same room with her, then at her feet. For the next eight months the man and woman sleep in the same bed but without sex, this time

---

*In an advanced adept who has trained in the rite of *maithuna*, the ability to "return the semen" is said to be gained. The male is trained to be able to draw the seminal fluid back into his body while at the same time drawing in the fluids of his partner.

of celibacy bringing about a comfortableness and an 'auton-omization' of physical sensuality. Here, the emphasis is on feeling, not genitality. Mastery of self-control is slowly learned as the husband becomes accustomed to the body of his bride. Once that has occurred, says Eliade, "He reaches a state of detachment where he neither desires her nor does he not de-sire her. He will have passed beyond the level of conscious-ness in which he demands personal or sensual gratification for its own sake."[4]

In *Island*, Aldous Huxley describes the ritual of *maithuna* as the regaining of the childhood paradise of unbounded sex-uality—nongenital, unfocused, and unlimited in its joy: "What we're born with, what we experience all through infancy and childhood is a sexuality that isn't concentrated on the geni-tals; it's a sexuality diffused through the whole organism. That's the paradise we inherit. But the paradise gets lost as the child grows up. Maithuna is the organized attempt to re-gain that paradise."[5]

Huxley adds that this heightened control does not involve the repression of sexual feelings, but "its perfect integration with the voluntary capacities of man."

Celibacy and Health

After an interview on the *Phil Donahue Show* with a man who had been celibate for four years, many of the women in the audience remarked how attractive he was and what a shame it was that this man was celibate. But what they didn't realize is that men who are in good health, celibate, and also com-fortable with being celibate (i.e., not straining or repressing their feelings) often develop a glow on their skin which we might associate with very good health. In India, this quality of the skin is attributed to *ojas*, a substance said to be pro-duced by the body that indicates a refined physiology and higher states of consciousness, and is also said to be one re-sult of celibacy in both men and women.

Says Jay Glaser, M.D., a medical researcher, "There's an idea that celibacy is good for health, but it's very difficult to measure because it's extremely subtle. The difficulty of doing research is further compounded by the fact that people who become celibate are generally also involved in a number of other unique lifestyles, including participation in religious orders."

The best study to date to test the value of celibacy for promoting good health was an analysis of the mortality rates and causes of death among Catholic priests between 1965 and 1977. Oddly enough, the study was looking for a possible link between celibacy and prostate cancer. However, to their surprise, the researchers found a 30 percent *lower* mortality rate from prostate and all form of cancer among the clerics than among the general population and a 15 percent lower death rate in general.[6]

There are a number of individuals in our society at present who are having to be celibate, for whom celibacy is a significant, health-maintaining measure, or for whom it is chosen out of anxiety. "The worried well" is the name given to people whose anxiety is produced by the fear of AIDS. Even those without reason to be fearful can be struck by this fear. It is certainly one major reason for the rise of celibacy in our society, even if it is not always the best basis for a healthy and comfortable experience of celibacy. Yet it should be recognized that the practice of celibacy may in turn help reduce stress. Celibacy—along with accurate information, stress reduction techniques, and various therapies—can significantly help allay the anxiety.

Any form of stress reduction is useful for those who have good reason to worry about AIDS, given the known relationship between stress and immune system functioning. Obviously physical stress takes its toll, but mental and emotional stress are equally debilitating. In fact, some researchers are persuaded that people who get AIDS are those who live or have lived under the most stressful emotional circumstances, whether caused by poverty or prejudice or both.

But even a promiscuous sex life can incur stress. Many of the "new celibates," both men and women, report that they experience a big difference between monogamous and promiscuous sex, in that the latter often seems far more draining emotionally. It may also be more draining physically, but that's a more elusive variable. The opportunity for foreign antigens to enter the body is of course always present. A lot of non-monogamous sex may require overactivity on the part of the immune system, brought on by a relatively constant state of alertness to invasion by foreign antibodies. On the other hand, it has been observed that having a long relationship with one sexual partner does not produce the need for constant monitoring; the physiology of one becomes familiar with the physiology of the other, and over time, both systems reach equilibrium and regain internal balance more easily after sex.

However it is incurred, physical and emotional stress reduces the ability of the immune system to maintain balance and thereby fight off disease. Conservation of energy is based on the principle of homeostasis—the law of balance—which operates throughout nature in such a way that whatever enemy comes along can be dealt with most efficiently. From this angle, it is best to have an immune system which conserves energy and which maintains itself in its least active state while no emergency is present. According to Dr. Glaser, a consultant at clinics in San Francisco and New York researching the benefits of AyurVeda in preventing AIDS and its use in the adjunctive and supportive care of AIDS patients, "There is definitely a positive benefit to conserving the immune reserve in order to deal with illness."

Dr. Glaser and his colleagues are exploring the effects of stress management and celibacy on a hormone associated with the immune system. This hormone, called dehydroepiandrosterone sulfate (DHEAS), is produced by the adrenal gland and varies in quantity with age. Found in very high levels in the fetus, it peaks around twenty to twenty-four years in both men and women and declines by approximately 15 percent each decade as we grow older. It increases acutely under duress and may function as a buffer to allow the body to quickly produce large quantities of stress-related hormones such as cortisol. However, because it can be depleted and because the body can't distinguish between real, life-threatening emergencies and our own manufactured stresses, we may unnecessarily lose that which we most need through the wear and tear of psychic stress. For example, if we worry for two weeks prior to surgery about that fearsome knife, we end up needlessly depleting our stress hormone reserve, weakening our overall immune system.

When the immune system gets out of balance, it either overreacts to the presence of a nonthreatening influence, such as pollens (resulting in illnesses such as allergies), or it inappropriately reacts against other functions in the body in autoimmune diseases (such as lupus). Researchers have found that the human immunodeficiency virus (HIV), which causes AIDS, is unique in that its effect is aggravated by stress, which causes the immune system to overreact, to crank away at a very high rate of energy until there is little or no immune reserve left to combat the intrusion of foreign antigens. "Paradoxically," says Dr. Glaser, "The AIDS virus [that is, HIV] flourishes best in the situation where the immune system is overactive."

The Healing Consequences of AIDS

> Reconciliation was a far more common scenario for AIDS patients and their families than abandonment ...there was talk of lovers abandoning their AIDS-stricken partners but the more commonly enacted stories were of unparalleled fidelity. There was also the bravery of these men facing an early death.
>
> ——RANDY SHILTS[7]

On a practical yet always courageous basis, most gay men realize they must take the AIDS test more than once to be sure of the result. They know they will have to endure the anxiety of taking it regularly for at least another six or seven years. But beyond that very real concern, by now most of them have known, on average, fifty people who have died of AIDS, and most have perhaps twenty friends who are sick with the AIDS virus. As one man expressed it:

> People simply don't talk about the implications of AIDS because no one wants to believe they saw it coming. I think what AIDS is really about is transcendence, but it's a pretty horrible way to get there. Most of us have had to dig down into what's real in order to find perspective. Otherwise it's unbearable. You find yourself in a perpetual state of mourning. You get over one loss and another comes along; you can never get away from it. I don't think you can live in that proximity to such suffering and not think what it means. Death is much easier to accept than watching these lovely people being compelled to suffer like that.

For some men, this experience means turning to a spiritual life and a spiritual practice which may include celibacy, not simply for the sake of safe sex, but for the sake of a larger purpose, to develop the kind of spiritual integration required for self-acceptance and the healing quality of love.

The following is an excerpt from an interview with one man who has found a spiritual path to help deal with the situation.

One Man's Path, 1988: An Interview with Robert, Age Forty-two, Set Designer and Opera Director Turned Zen Monk

"I have been gay since I was eighteen. From the time I graduated from the University of Michigan in 1967, I witnessed and was a participant in the growth of the gay community. I believe this orientation automatically produces a certain amount of stress for any person who has to deal with prejudice and social and self-hatred. I was lucky because I have always had a good relationship with my parents, so I was able to come out to them early on, and we have remained close. I've always been basically a loner, even though I have very dear friends. The whole idea of finding fulfillment in another person has never made sense to me. Over the years, I've had affairs but no long-term partner nor a desire for one.

"I'd say I've had an immensely blessed life in that everything I've ever wanted has come to me easily. As an opera set designer, my favorite experience was standing in an empty theater at the starting point where anything is possible and seeing my creation unfold from there. Practicing my meditation makes me equally happy in that way. It is teaching me how to love in the deepest sense.

"I thought about celibacy long before AIDS. It was my reaction to sex in general. I've always felt that sex is a snare, a complication. It always seemed to be something that confused my life. From my early thirties, I've thought about being free from sex. The bars and that whole game which I did for many years seemed to reduce me to a set of responses and to a person whom I didn't like very much. I've always been aware that just having sex without a real relationship is not very evolutionary. I remember ten years ago lying in a room at the baths and thinking, 'This is simply not healthy.'

"About three and a half years ago, I was diagnosed HIV positive. Right around that time, I started a practice of Zen meditation, sitting for about forty minutes to one hour every morning. It is my belief that it has saved my life. My blood test reports changed and continue to be negative.

"I've only been occasionally with one lover over the past two years (safely, of course) and have become increasingly celibate quite naturally. The first time I was totally celibate (without masturbating) was for fifty days during my first stay at the Zen monastery. It felt very comfortable to me. All in all, I think there is probably some association between my health and celibacy. During my three-year training period, I will have the option of celibacy, and although I think it will be difficult, I want to pursue that option.

"I find that many of my friends have retreated into a kind of 'get through the day' routine. I hope for more for them. I never strongly recommend my new way of life and my new 'profession' to friends, but I do feel I practice the meditation for them as well as for myself. It's the deepest positive response I can find to what's going on. Most of the gay men I know have very strong spiritual tendencies and in another age would have been in the church or active in other celibate spiritual traditions which are there for people who don't make families. At this point, I would not understand life or good health without a spiritual practice."

This desire to promote health and healing on a deeper and truer level is apparently a growing phenomenon among gay men facing AIDS. In San Francisco, perhaps the hardest-hit gay community, there are resources such as the Hartford Street Zen Center and the AyurVeda Health and Education Resources Center offering integrative, health-oriented services.

The monks who run the Zen Center have a hospice for AIDS patients called *Maitri* (which means "friendliness" in Sanskrit) which offers a a settled environment and practical knowledge for preparing for a spiritual death, while providing a valuable inner and outer support system which comes directly out of their spiritual practice and commitment. Says the head priest, Issan Dorsey: "If I hadn't been practicing Buddhism, I wouldn't have been so deeply involved in the AIDS crisis....The truth is so close to us that it makes it easier to take our energy 'glue' out of our plans and ideas, and reside instead in our breathing."[8]

The Indian system of medicine known as AyurVeda is said to help reestablish the perfect functioning between the mind and body so that the body's own intelligence can trigger the healing response and promote good health. Says Deepak Chopra, M.D., president of the American Association of Ayur-Vedic Medicine, "Through thought, you can manufacture healing chemicals in your own brain which are thousands of times more powerful than any drug you can buy or any disease you might have."

According to its director, Craig Perrinjaquet, M.D., "The AyurVeda Health and Education Resources Center offers patients with AIDS and various other kinds of illnesses profound daily routines for a healthy life, using two approaches: One is internal, through the daily practice of Transcendental Meditation (TM), which serves to strengthen the immune system by eliminating stress," and, says Perrinjaquet, which "helps the person to get in touch directly with the self-referral value of consciousness, the integrating principle of mind/body coordination, so patients know intuitively what to do for themselves.... It's obvious that when your awareness is subtle, you are much more alert to when you feel weakened or drained by any activity. It's your mind and body telling you something important and you can take care of it easily and quickly." The other approach used is external, following individually prescribed AyurVedic health guidelines which focus on diet, the use of beneficial nonpharmacological products, and exercise to help people deal in a comfortable way with changes in their physical lives.

Given the enormity of the problems AIDS is presenting, these and other important health options are much more likely to help turn the societal tide toward healing and curing than toward fear, which creates isolation, lack of acceptance, and deprivation of the healing power of love. It is perhaps ironic that the fierce need to deter, contain, and cure this disease will bring the opportunity for much deeper healing in our society and also bring respect for the subjective forms of health and spiritual integration long missing for many of us. As one man observes: "In a strange way, I think that many of these men who are dealing with AIDS are becoming secular spiritual teachers to show other people a lot of things about life."

A Modern Outlook on Celibacy

There really aren't any basic rules for how to be celibate in Western culture, nor any definitive techniques. And there seems to be a much less sophisticated body of experiential knowledge in the West than in the East with regard to sexual functioning. According to sex researchers Gagnon and Simon, "work on increasing 'voluntary' control of sexual responses ...is beginning only at the present moment."

Celibacy itself is currently considered a technique for enhancing sexual response. In fact, it is regarded as the best cure for impotence. It works because the body immediately starts to normalize its functioning and allows sexual response to develop comfortably from the "rest" state, when one's physiology is maximally prepared for activity. It is interesting to consider the possibility that impotence may be the body's way to take the rest it needs—physiologically imposed. Yet, impotence differs from celibacy because it is not an integrated state of functioning but rather indicates a breakdown in mind-body coordination—the mind commands and the body does not obey.

It is not surprising that celibacy revitalizes sexuality by giving the body the opportunity to rest. But, at the same time, it also revitalizes *all* parts of the body. It's a physical trade-off. Because the body functions as a system in which the workings of each part affect all others, celibacy changes not only sexual functioning but the entire physiology and total body functioning as well. By eliminating sex from daily experience, the body can become open to other physiological ways to expend the conserved energy, which include mental and emotional changes, experienced as greater vitality; more mental clarity and focusing ability; more refined perception; and more profound feelings of love. Overall, says Haich, "My body calms down...yet it lives with much greater intensity and has much greater potency than the body of [one] who is still in the grip of sexuality."

Celibacy can help create a wholeness in mind-body functioning that contributes to a more equitable balance of physical, mental, and emotional functions. Keeping in mind that one is in a sense "donating" one's sexual energy to various other endeavors helps to promote a happy private experience of its value.

It is also useful to remind oneself that being celibate is an alternate way to love, even to make love. One can learn to touch nonpossessively, without a future goal—and to make love nonsexually, unmotivated by the need for sexual gratification. Being aware of one's sexuality and thinking about it as a passive state rather than an active one helps place the emphasis on a generalized feeling of love and well-being rather than on a localized response.

And, finally, it is clear that although one can decide to be celibate, a certain degree of consciousness must be present both to make that choice and to maintain it. No methods for celibacy are more important than this. And if one wants to, one can easily find a useful mental technique for developing consciousness with the accompanying benefits for body and mind.

It would seem that being a life celibate might in some ways be easier for a person than becoming celibate on and off. Life celibacy is a very different reality which usually becomes manifest at an early age as part of a larger spiritual commitment. But for most people choosing celibacy after a number of years of a more sexually active life, there's always an active decision to make until the experience of being celibate becomes more a habit. Living in a stimulating urban environment which heavily promotes sex even as it campaigns against it makes the initial choice to be celibate a little unique. So in the beginning, there has to be some vigilance. But as one pursues this path over time, a kind of easiness and relaxation sets in as one experiences that it isn't really uncomfortable or unnatural to be celibate.

In this light, perhaps the most significant thing we can say about the practice of celibacy is that it has to be cultivated. One does not often move swiftly from a very active sexual life to a nonsexually active life. The habits of sex cultured in our physiology over the years are no doubt powerful. Yet individuals who have chosen to be celibate remark on how natural it feels once their attention is deployed in that direction. With this attitude in mind, it should never really feel like deprivation, more like growing toward a kind of inner fullness.

In a recent curriculum developed to introduce the concept of celibacy to high school students, the understanding of sex as a cover-up for our real need for love is emphasized:

> Sex is often a disguised desire for acceptance, love and security. When we feel these desires, we don't have to fulfill them in sexual intercourse. We can feel the same kind of love, acceptance, and security when we rechannel our energy to some other good purpose.... It takes practice to learn this kind of self-control, but we can. And the more self-control we have, the better we feel about ourselves. We won't be slaves to our feelings and impulses. We'll have more respect for ourselves and we'll probably earn more respect from others.[9]

All true, but the idea of self-control seems at best burdensome. No one should be celibate by inducing strain and stress in his or her physiology. In fact such strain could result in a worse situation than having sex. The more helpful attitude might be: "I am not controlling anything; rather I am expressing something, a realization of who I am and what I want."

In most cases, celibacy represents an inward turning of one's attention away from a need to be fulfilled outside oneself. In this sense, it is rarely experienced as a single mode of behavior; it generally goes along with other inner-directed behavior.

When you have a deep love relationship, it's easier to be celibate with that person because celibacy comes out of that connection. You can flow together in your hearts. If you don't have real communication and a real heartful connection with your partner, you'll tend to look to the sexual connection to provide the intimacy. And it's very difficult to be celibate in a relationship unless you have those intimate connected feelings well-established. We might even say that celibacy which promotes real intimacy between two people is only possible in the closest relationships, not in the most distant.

SOME GUIDELINES ON HOW TO BE CELIBATE

What follows is a way to think about some of the advantages and possible situations that may arise from being celibate today.

- Celibacy is most naturally and smoothly maintained with a relaxed attitude both toward yourself and toward others.

- It's simplest if you start out being comfortable with your own body; your desires will be there, and they will feel perfectly natural, but you don't necessarily have to act on them. In a little while, they will probably subside.

- Learn to treat other people's sexual interests lightly but respectfully. If someone is flirting with you, and you feel uptight as a result, you are going to feel more uncomfortable than if you are just easy with it. You don't want to make them feel uncomfortable. This easiness will dissolve any sexual tension between you.

- Always know who you are to yourself. Just as when you're on a diet, you should feel so secure inside that you can sit and have tea with your friends in a pastry shop without feeling an unbearable desire to eat pastry. You are ultimately doing this not as a form of deprivation but because it gives you a deeper level of satisfaction—you are giving yourself something you want.

- At times, physical, nonsexual touching and being touched is an essential nourishment for nearly everyone. No one practicing celibacy should feel that physical contact with others is entirely taboo. All of us need this, and if understood and appreciated simply for what it is, not as a forbidden thing, it even helps to maintain celibacy.

- Think of it as a vacation. During a vacation, you can expect to feel more rested, more relaxed, less pressured, more open to new experiences. You can expect the same from celibacy.

- During a vacation, you try new activities that you don't ordinarily try at home. During a period of celibacy, there are some things you can do that you can't when you're involved sexually:

  You can express all your *other* feelings.

  You can plunge into your work or your other interests without distraction or guilt.

  You can dine with a friend and (1) eat as much as you want, (2) meet someone else afterward, (3) go home alone.

  You can become intimate friends with your intimates without negotiations.

  You can fall in love all over again, enjoy romance, court and be courted.

- Enjoy yourself. You'll probably have a lot of energy for a lot of things you've been thinking about doing.

- If sexual thoughts come up, don't attend to them. There's no sense being celibate if you make it a big strain for yourself. Thinking about sex constantly can be just as sexual as having sex. And not as rewarding.

- You can be celibate for as long a time as you want
  to be—for a month, a year, or more. When you do
  return from vacation, everything will look fresh and
  new again.

If and when you stop being celibate, sex will have something new to offer you. Not only because you've been away, but because you are more settled within yourself. Or you can continue being on vacation if you're enjoying it. In either case, you can count on some very profound personal benefits to have occurred.

ACCEPTING CELIBACY

When we are taught the "rules" for sex, we need to learn not only what is socially acceptable and what might not be, but also that sex has an extended value that goes well beyond both its pleasure and procreative functions. The way to learn everything we ever wanted to know about sex is in the context of *full* knowledge of its range of expression—which must include celibacy. If we all have the potential to be celibate, then it is really a matter of finding out about and accepting this aspect of being sexual along with the active aspect of sex.

Whether celibacy is practiced under the guidance of a particular spiritual community or in the bedroom of a married couple, it is beginning to emerge in our society as a useful and positive vehicle to further personal growth for a number of people today. That this emergence is occurring in the midst of so many other social changes can lead to a great deal of speculation as to its real causes. But there are three trends in particular that may be most important in understanding today's new celibacy. One is obviously to avoid the dangers of disease. Another is the need to balance the uncomfortably heavy social focus on sexuality that continues to bombard this society—an overdoing for which two hundred years of sexual repression may no longer be a good excuse. The third is the steadily rising interest in spiritual development. Celibacy may be one way for the individual and the society to resolve and integrate all these needs.

But if it is a social movement at all, it is a very private one. True, the new celibates are beginning to find and support each other....They may even be old lovers reunited on a new basis. But there is no celibate "movement" as yet—no group of advocates on street corners with STOP signs. The men and women interviewed for this book were extremely private about their changed or changing sexuality. They may be pioneers, but they are not really ready to establish this new sexual frontier alone.

Gagnon and Simon found in their research on socialized sexuality that "being the first to change [sexually] means dealing with certain kinds of anxieties and ambivalences." And Campbell observed that "no single person or couple can innovate a new style of sexual behavior, for sexuality is a complicated social phenomenon and always presupposes at least a minimally representative community as its basic unit." If this is the case, then we can assume that the practice of celibacy has a certain basic unit of social acceptance already or there would be no possibility for its support in our society at this time.

What we are seeing now is a deepening of societal needs which can only be met by the deepening strength and increased creativity, intelligence, and happiness of each of us. As we grow in these values, all aspects of our development have to keep up and be integrated with each other. It is likely that this is why celibacy is surfacing—not for all of us—but for many who are ready for a more intimate, more flexible experience of love and a more balanced approach to living fulfilled, progressive lives.

Notes

PREFACE

1. *Newsweek*, March 14, 1988.

CHAPTER 1

1. Randy Shilts, *And the Band Played On: Politics, People and The AIDS Epidemic*, St. Martin's Press, New York, 1987, p. 377.

2. Ibid., pp. 89, 484.

3. *Newsweek*, June 23, 1986, p. 25.

4. Personal interview, April 12, 1988.

5. Linda Wolfe, "The New Sexual Realism," *Ladies Home Journal*, April 1987, p. 171.

6. Barbara Ehrenreich, Elizabeth Hess, and Gloria Jacobs, "Remaking Love: The Real Sexual Revolution," *Ms.*, July 1986, p. 82.

7. *Ebony*, November 1987, pp. 52–56.

8. Rae Corelli, "Running the Risks in Casual Affairs," *Maclean's*, January 4, 1988, pp. 52–54; also John Barber, "A New View of Sexuality," *Maclean's*, January 5, 1987, p. 70.

9. Srully Blotnick, *Otherwise Engaged: The Private Lives of Successful Career Women*, Penguin Books, New York, 1986.

10. *People,* March 14, 1988, p. 105.

11. *Ebony,* November 1987, p. 54.

12. *Ibid.,* p. 54.

13. Carin Rubinstein and Carol Tavris, "Survey Results," *Redbook,* September 1987, pp. 148–149, 214–216.

14. ABC News, Nightline Edition, January 25, 1988.

15. *People,* March 14, 1988, p. 108.

16. *Ibid.*

17. Shilts, op. cit., p. 589.

18. David Streitfeld, "The New Sexual Revolution," *Washington Post,* April 11, 1986, Section C5; also Wolfe, *Ladies Home Journal,* April 1987, p. 168.

19. *People,* March 14, 1988, p. 105.

20. Wolfe, *Ladies Home Journal,* April 1987, p. 168.

21. *Ibid.*

22. Barber, *Maclean's,* January 5, 1987, p. 70.

23. Streitfeld, *Washington Post,* April 11, 1986, Section C5.

24. Frances FitzGerald, "The Castro: II," *New Yorker,* July 28, 1986, p. 61.

25. Randy Shilts, personal interview, April 12, 1988.

26. Anonymous, personal interview, February 20, 1988.

27. Craig Perrinjaquet, M.D., personal interview, July 5, 1988.

28. *Ebony,* November 1987, p. 52.

29. *People,* March 14, 1988, p. 105.

30. Barber, *Maclean's,* January 5, 1987, p. 70.

31. Gary Hanauer, "Turning on to Turning Off," *Penthouse,* January 1986, pp. 65–71.

32. "Virginity Regained," *Harper's,* April 1987, p. 20.

33. *Newsweek,* August 25, 1986.

34. Georgia Dullea, "A Lack of Sexual Desire Emerges as a Contemporary Condition," *New York Times*, May 1, 1978, p. A18.

35. Bertrand Russell, *Marriage and Morals*, Bantam Books, New York, 1968, pp. 9–10. First published in 1929.

36. Abraham Maslow, *Motivation and Personality*, Harper & Row, New York, 1970, pp. 187–188.

37. Theodore Cole, M.D., *Medical Aspects of Human Sexuality*, June 1976.

38. Elisabeth Haich, *Sexual Energy and Yoga*, ASI Publishers, New York, 1975, p. 52.

39. "How Our Passions and Hatreds Are Aroused," *San Francisco Chronicle*, September 18, 1978, p. 1.

40. Barbara Seaman, *Free and Female: The Sex Life of the Contemporary Woman*, Coward, McCann, New York, 1972, p. 191.

41. Michael Volin and Nancy Phelan, *Sex and Yoga*, Harper & Row, New York, 1967, p. 23.

42. H. J. Campbell, *The Pleasure Areas: A New Theory of Behavior*, Delacorte Press, New York, 1973, pp. 282, 292.

CHAPTER 2

1. Barbara W. Tuchman, *A Distant Mirror: The Calamitous Fourteenth Century*, Alfred A. Knopf, New York, 1978, p. 212.

2. Sister M. Roberta, "A Sister Considers Chastity," *America*, April 10, 1965.

3. Joseph D. Wade, *Chastity, Sexuality and Personal Hang-Ups*, Alba House, New York, 1971.

4. *1988 Catholic Almanac.*

5. Paul M. Conner, *Celibate Love*, Our Sunday Visitor, Huntington, Ind., 1979, pp. 13–14.

6. *Newsweek*, August 25, 1986.

7. Anonymous, personal interview, 1979.

8. Joe K. Adams, "The Love Taboo," in Herbert Otto (ed.), *Love Today: A New Exploration*, Association Press, New York, 1972, p. 32.

9. A. C. Kinsey et al., *Sexual Behavior in the Human Female*, Saunders, Philadelphia, 1953, p. 625.

10. Charles Fracchia, *Living Together Alone: The New American Monasticism*, Harper & Row, San Francisco, 1979, pp. 124–125.

CHAPTER 3

1. Joe K. Adams, "The Love Taboo," in Herbert Otto (ed.), *Love Today: A New Exploration*, Association Press, New York, 1972, p. 32.

2. William Masters and Virginia Johnson, *The Pleasure Bond*, Little, Brown, Boston, 1975, pp. 173–174.

3. Peter Koestenbaum, *Existential Sexuality: Choosing to Love*, Prentice-Hall, Englewood Cliffs, N.J., 1974, pp. 17–18.

4. Abraham Maslow, "Love in Healthy People," in Ashley Montagu (ed.), *The Practice of Love*, Prentice-Hall, Englewood Cliffs, N.J., 1975, pp. 108–109.

5. Herbert W. Richardson, *Nun, Witch, Playmate: The Americanization of Sex*, Harper & Row, New York, 1971, pp. 35–36.

6. Elisabeth Haich, *Sexual Energy and Yoga*, ASI Publishers, New York, 1975, p. 101.

CHAPTER 4

1. John Davenport, *Curiosities of Erotic Physiology*, Robin Hood House, New York, 1932.

2. A. C. Kinsey et al., *Sexual Behavior in the Human Female*, Saunders, Philadelphia, 1953, p. 612.

3. Hugo Beigel, "Romantic Love," in Ashley Montagu (ed.), *The Practice of Love*, Prentice-Hall, Englewood Cliffs, N.J., 1975, p. 130.

4. Interview by Robert Levering, *San Francisco Bay Guardian*, November 23, 1978.

Chapter 5

1. Bertrand Russell, *Marriage and Morals*, Bantam Books, New York, 1968, p. 17.

2. Diana Trilling in Enid Harlow, "Sexual Liberation Doesn't Always Mean Freedom," *Working Woman*, June 1977, p. 53.

3. Barbara Seaman, *Free and Female: The Sex Life of the Contemporary Woman*, Coward, McCann, New York, 1972, p. 210.

4. *Discover*, December 1986, pp. 11–12.

5. Shere Hite, *The Hite Report*, Macmillan, New York, 1976, p. 337.

6. June Singer, *Androgyny: Towards a New Theory of Sexuality*, Doubleday Anchor, Garden City, N.Y., 1976, pp. 318–319.

7. Hite, op. cit., p. 205.

8. Helen Singer Kaplan, *The New Sex Therapy*, Brunner/Mazel, New York, 1974, p. 111.

9. Betty Holcomb, "The Case for Being Celibate," *Essence*, December 1985, p. 71.

10. Elissa Malcohn, "Notes on Celibate Bisexuality," *Celibate Woman Journal*, vol. 3, no. 2, February 1987, p. 19.

11. Martha Allen, "A Perspective on the Celibate Lifestyle," *Celibate Woman Journal*, March 1986, p. 4.

Chapter 6

1. Ellen Frank and Carol Andersen, "How Important Is Sex to a Happy Marriage?" *Family Circle Magazine*, March 13, 1979.

2. Philip Blumstein and Pepper Schwartz, *American Couples*, Random House, New York, 1983, pp. 201, 205–206.

3. Bertrand Russell, *Marriage and Morals*, Bantam Books, New York, 1968, p. 51.

4. Margery Rothgeb, "Cycles and Celibacy," *Celibate Woman Journal*, vol. 2, no. 2, January 1985, p. 32.

CHAPTER 7

1. Julian Huxley, "The Direction of Human Development," in Ashley Montagu (ed.), *The Practice of Love*, Prentice-Hall, Englewood Cliffs, N.J., 1975, p. 172.

2. June Singer, *Androgyny: Toward a New Theory of Sexuality*, Doubleday Anchor, Garden City, N.Y., 1976, p. 270.

3. H. J. Campbell, *The Pleasure Areas: A New Theory of Behavior*, Delacorte Press, New York, 1973, p. 208.

4. Sigmund Freud in Irving Singer, *The Nature of Love: Plato to Luther*, Random House, New York, 1966, p. 271.

5. Mary S. Calderone, "Sexuality—A Creative Force," in Herbert Otto (ed.), *The New Sexuality*, Science and Behavior Books, Palo Alto, Calif., 1971, pp. 269–270.

CHAPTER 8

1. Randy Shilts, *And the Band Played On: Politics, People and the AIDS Epidemic*, St. Martin's Press, New York, p. 103.

2. Bertrand Russell, *Marriage and Morals*, Bantam Books, New York, 1968, p. 27.

3. Elisabeth Haich, *Sexual Energy and Yoga*, ASI Publishers, New York, 1975, pp. 130–131.

4. Mircea Eliade, *Yoga, Immortality and Freedom*, Pantheon, New York, 1958, p. 254.

5. Aldous Huxley, *Island*, Harper, New York, 1962, p. 137.

6. *Journal of Surgical Oncology*, vol. 17, no. 2, 1981, pp. 129–133.

7. Shilts, op. cit., p. 356.

8. *New Yorker*, June 13, 1988, p. 24.

9. "Virginity Regained," *Harper's Magazine*, April 1987, p. 20.

Bibliography

Arieti, Silvano, and James A. Arieti: *Love Can Be Found*, Harcourt Brace Jovanovich, New York, 1977.

Bailey, D. S.: *Sexual Relations in Christian Thought*, Harper, New York, 1959.

Beigel, Hugo: "Romantic Love," in Ashley Montagu (ed.), *The Practice of Love*, Prentice-Hall, Englewood Cliffs, N.J., 1975.

Bianchi, Eugene: "America as Monastery," *Commonweal*, March 1, 1974, pp. 530–531.

Blofeld, John: *The Secret and the Sublime: Taoist Mysteries and Magic*, Dutton, New York, 1973.

Blotnick, Srully: *Otherwise Engaged: The Private Lives of Successful Career Women*, Penguin Books, New York, 1986.

Blumstein, Philip, and Pepper Schwartz: *American Couples*, Random House, New York, 1983.

Burrows, Millar: *Burrows on the Dead Sea Scrolls*, Baker Books, Grand Rapids, Mich., 1978.

Campbell, H. J.: *The Pleasure Areas: A New Theory of Behavior*, Delacorte Press, New York, 1973.

Chaucard, Paul: *Our Need of Love*, P. J. Kenedy, New York, 1968.

Colton, Helen: *Sex after the Sexual Revolution*, Association Press, New York, 1972.

Eliade, Mircea: *Yoga, Immortality and Freedom*, Pantheon Books, New York, 1958.

Fellman, Sheldon, and Paul Neimark: *The Virile Man*, Stein & Day, New York, 1976.

Fracchia, Charles: *Living Together Alone: The New American Monasticism*, Harper & Row, San Francisco, 1979.

Freud, Sigmund: *Civilization and Its Discontents*, W. W. Norton, New York, 1962.

Fromm, Erich: *The Art of Loving*, Harper & Row, New York, 1962.

Gagnon, John H., and William Simon: *Sexual Conduct: The Social Sources of Human Sexuality*, Aldine, Chicago, 1973.

Goergen, Donald: *The Sexual Celibate*, Seabury, New York, 1974.

Gould, Arthur, and F. L. DuBois: *The Science of Sex Regeneration*, Advanced Thought Co., Chicago, 1911.

Haich, Elisabeth: *Sexual Energy and Yoga*, ASI Publishers, New York, 1975.

Hite, Shere: *The Hite Report*, Macmillan, New York, 1976.

Hunt, Morton: *Sexual Behavior in the 1970s*, Playboy Press, Chicago, 1974.

Hurcombe, Linda (ed.): *Sex and God: Some Varieties of Women's Religious Experiences*, Routledge and Kegan Paul, New York and London, 1987.

Huxley, Aldous: *Island*, Harper, New York, 1962.

Kinsey, A. C., W. B. Pomeroy, and C. E. Martin: *Sexual Behavior in the Human Female*, Saunders, Philadelphia, 1953.

———, ———, and ———: *Sexual Behavior in the Human Male*, Saunders, Philadelphia, 1948.

Koestenbaum, Peter: *Existential Sexuality: Choosing to Love*, Prentice-Hall, Englewood Cliffs, N.J., 1974.

Laski, Marghanita: *Ecstasy: A Study of Some Secular and Religious Experiences*, Greenwood Press, Westport, Conn., 1968.

Lea, Henry C.: *History of Sacerdotal Celibacy in the Christian Church*, Watts, London, 1932.

Lederer, William J., and Don D. Jackson: *The Mirages of Marriage*, W. W. Norton, New York, 1968.

Lewis, C. S.: *The Four Loves*, Collins, London, 1960.

Maslow, A.: "Love in Healthy People," in Ashley Montagu (ed.), *The Practice of Love*, Prentice-Hall, Englewood Cliffs, N.J., 1975.

——: *Motivation and Personality*, Harper & Row, New York, 1970.

Masters, William, and Virginia Johnson: *Human Sexual Response*, Little, Brown, Boston, 1966.

—— and ——: *The Pleasure Bond: A New Look at Sexuality and Commitment*, Little, Brown, Boston, 1975.

May, Rollo: *Love and Will*, W. W. Norton, New York, 1969.

Menninger, Walter: *Happiness without Sex and Other Things Too Good to Miss*, Sheed, Andrews and McMeel, New York, 1976.

Meyer, J. J.: *Sexual Life in Ancient India*, Barnes & Noble, New York, 1953.

Money, John, and Patricia Tucker: *Sexual Signatures*, Little, Brown, Boston, 1975.

Montagu, Ashley (ed.): *The Practice of Love*, Prentice-Hall, Englewood Cliffs, N.J., 1975.

——: *Touching: The Human Significance of Skin*, Harper & Row, New York, 1972.

Otto, Herbert A.: *Love Today: A New Exploration*, Association Press, New York, 1972.

——: *The New Sexuality*, Science and Behavior Books, Palo Alto, Calif., 1971.

Richardson, Herbert W.: *Nun, Witch, Playmate: The Americanization of Sex*, Harper & Row, New York, 1971.

Roberta, Sister M.: "A Sister Considers Chastity," *America*, April 10, 1965.

Rosenbaum, Jean B.: "A Psychoanalyst's Case for Celibacy," *Catholic World*, May 1967.

Rosner, Fred: *Sex Ethics in the Writings of Moses Maimonides*, Bloch Publishing Co., New York, 1974.

Rugoff, Milton: *Prudery and Passion: Sexuality in Victorian America*, Putnam, New York, 1971.

Russell, Bertrand: *Marriage and Morals*, Liveright, 1929; Bantam Books, New York, 1968.

Sadler, William A.: *Existence and Love: A New Approach in Existential Phenomenology*, Scribner, New York, 1970.

Seaman, Barbara: *Free and Female: The Sex Life of the Contemporary Woman*, Coward, McCann, New York, 1972.

Shilts, Randy: *And the Band Played On: Politics, People and the AIDS Epidemic*, St. Martin's Press, New York, 1987.

Singer, Irving: *The Nature of Love: Plato to Luther*, Random House, New York, 1966.

Singer, June: *Androgyny: Toward a New Theory of Sexuality*, Anchor Press/Doubleday, Garden City, N.Y., 1976.

Slater, Philip: *Footholds: Understanding the Shifting Sexual and Family Tensions in Our Culture*, Dutton, New York, 1977.

Sullivan, Harry S.: *Interpersonal Theory of Psychiatry*, W. W. Norton, New York, 1953.

Teilhard de Chardin, Pierre: *Human Energy*, Harcourt Brace Jovanovich, New York, 1970.

Volin, Michael, and Nancy Phelan: *Sex and Yoga*, Harper & Row, New York, 1967.

Wade, Joseph D.: *Chastity, Sexuality and Personal Hang-Ups*, Alba House, New York, 1971.

Zilbergeld, Bernard: *Male Sexuality: A Guide to Personal Fulfillment*, Little, Brown, Boston, 1977.

Catalog

If you are interested in a list of fine Paperback
books, covering a wide range of subjects
and interests, send your name and address,
requesting your free catalog, to:

McGraw-Hill Paperbacks
11 West 19th Street
New York, N.Y. 10011